"Around the world, church-planting strategi
graphical area to languages to people-grou
cross-culture; from international to national;
becoming a people's movement. I believe tha
ers a "global" vision and strengthen their miss   — p.a.u
churches among unreached people groups in one's own land and culture,
and beyond. I am sure this book will become a strong force to move both
individuals and churches to join this great movement."

—Bishop John Gollapalli, Free Methodist Church of India

"The studies contained in this volume provide a window into the joys
and challenges of church planting, as well as a glimpse into the creativity, commitment, and willingness to risk that marks the men and women
involved in this work. This is an important read for anyone engaged in
evangelism and the creation of new places to reach new people with the
gospel."

—Kimberly D. Reisman, Executive Director,
World Methodist Evangelism

"This was a strategic gathering of denominational and church leaders
with extraordinary breadth and experience, and it was truly humbling to
see all that God is doing through them. I came away inspired, encouraged, and challenged to pray, 'Thy Kingdom Come' with renewed determination."

—The Rt Revd Ric Thorpe, Bishop of Islington

"Asbury Seminary's Global Church Planting Summit was an incredible
global gathering of leaders that highlighted many of the future challenges
and opportunities for global church planting. We heard incredible stories
from church planters from every corner of the globe—all with the common heart of proclaiming the truth of the Bible to every nation. I gained
many useful insights and left fantastically encouraged."

—Christian Selvaratnam, Head of Alpha UK

"The world is coming to our cities in beautiful new ways. Asbury's Global Church Planting Summit has provided a unique forum for exchanging fresh ideas on how to engage in this present Pentecost moment."

—Rev Graham Singh, Executive Director, Church Planting Canada

"We hope this book is a gift to others who share a common desire to see church planting continue to bear fruit in diverse cultural contexts. As World Christianity continues to blossom around the globe, we need more books such as this one, which take the reader by the hand into the incredible diversity and beauty of global church planting. At the conclusion of this book it's easy to marvel at God's mission in the world, and how he's accomplishing it through the planting of congregations as witnesses to the activity of the Father, Son, and Holy Spirit."

—Gregg Oakesson, Dean of the School of
World Missions, Asbury Seminary

GLOBAL VOICES

STORIES OF CHURCH PLANTING FROM AROUND THE WORLD

EDITED BY WINFIELD BEVINS
FOREWORD BY TIMOTHY C. TENNENT

CHURCH
PLANTING
INITIATIVE

To Bill and Phyllis Johnson
In gratitude for your passion and support
for global church planting

CONTENTS

CONTRIBUTORS

Dr. Winfield Bevins is Director of Church Planting at Asbury Theological Seminary. He is a seasoned practitioner who has helped plant churches and has been instrumental in launching several church-planting networks. He is the author of several books including *Church Planting Revolution* and *Marks of a Movement*.

Dr. Paul Chang has served in a seminary in Beijing since December 2015 and trains and teaches Chinese mission volunteers and supports the Mission China movement to Korean and other churches.

Dr. Ricardo and Elizabeth Gómez serve as missionary educators in Medellín, Colombia. Ricardo is professor of pastoral theology at the Fundación Universitaria Seminario Bíbilico de Colombia and oversees the theological education of Free Methodist pastors throughout Latin America, as well as a local church planting movement in Medellín, Colombia.

Rev. Wayne Hilsden is the co-founder of King of Kings Community in Jerusalem as well as Israel College of the Bible in Netanya and has initiated the planting of several congregations in various parts of Israel.

Dr. W. Jay Moon is Professor of Church Planting and Evangelism and Co-director of the Office of Faith, Work, and Economics at Asbury Theological Seminary in Wilmore, Kentucky. He previously taught at Sioux Falls Seminary and also served in Ghana, West Africa, with SIM.

Rev. Dr. Patrick L. Murunga is currently the Principal of Africa Theological Seminary (ATS) in Kitale, Kenya, and recently retired from 25 years of full-time pastoral responsibilities. Upon retirement, he was elected and serves as the Nairobi Region director of the Nairobi churches of Africa Gospel Church.

Dr. Gregg Okesson is Dean, E. Stanley Jones School of World Mission and Evangelism at Asbury Theological Seminary, and has authored numerous articles and serves on the editorial committee for the *Africa Journal of Evangelical Theology* and the *Africa Study Bible*. He is the author of *Re-Imaging Modernity* (Wipf & Stock, 2012) and co-author of *Advocating for Justice* (Baker Academic, 2016). He is currently writing a book on *Public Missiology*, under contract with Baker Academic.

Rev. Christian Selvaratnam is an ordained priest and Pioneer Minister in the Church of England. He works as the Head of Alpha UK, supporting nearly ten thousand churches in the United Kingdom who run the Alpha course and associated ministries, and is also the leader of G2, an innovative church plant in York.

Rev. Graham Singh is the Rector of St. Jax Montréal and Executive Director of Church Planting Canada.

Dr. Timothy C. Tennent is President of Asbury Theological Seminary and Professor of World Christianity at the school. He is the author of several books, including *Building Christianity on Indian Foundations, Christianity at the Religious Roundtable, Theology in the Context of World Christianity: How the Global Church is Influencing the Way We Think About and Discuss Theology*, and *Invitation to World Missions: A Missiology for the 21st Century*.

Rev. Clint Ussher is an ordained minister of the Wesleyan Methodist Church of New Zealand (WMCNZ) and the founding pastor of the Well, which is a strategic church plant of the denomination.

Rev. John Varghese serves as the General Secretary of CEA, India, and pastors a local church in Delhi. His case study looks at the Christian Evangelistic Assemblies (CEA), a North India-based (Hindi belt) church-planting organization that was registered with the Government of India as a charitable society in 1994.

FOREWORD

As a part of our strategic commitment to church planting, Asbury Theological Seminary has been seeking to learn as much as we can about what God is doing around the world in raising up fresh expressions of his church. On June 26-28, 2017, we held our first global church-planting conference at Nazarene Theological College in Manchester, England. We brought together more than sixty church planters from a diversity of contexts around the world for a time of mutual sharing and listening to case studies. We heard case studies from Jerusalem to India, from Columbia to China, from Kenya to New Zealand, and many more. Every day felt like unwrapping an array of new, precious gifts from God, each of which displayed his glory and reminded us all that the emergence of a new wave of vibrant, global Christianity is one of the most remarkable signs of God's work in the world today. What God is doing globally is much bigger than any one person, denomination, or global strategizing.

Those of us who had the privilege of attending the summit went away with a fresh sense of awe and wonder at God's marvelous work. It was like the *missio Dei*, or mission of God, was being revealed to us not as a mere theological category but enfleshed in real-life contexts. We all agreed that these stories and case studies needed to be shared with the wider church—and this book is the fruit of that dream.

One of the big themes you will discover in this carefully selected survey is that there is a big difference between a *Post-Christian* West and a *Post-Western* Christianity. The case studies from New Zealand, Canada, and the United Kingdom reveal particular challenges for those representing the gospel in their contexts of an emerging post-Christian culture. In contrast, the case studies from Kenya, India, China, and Columbia reveal the promise of a whole new phase of Post-Western Christian vibrancy. The case study in Jerusalem reveals the unique challenges of planting an international church at the crossroads of the world's three major monotheistic religions. The breadth and depth of what these case studies witness to is truly stunning. Yet this is just a tiny sampling of what God is doing globally. May these case studies awaken you to many of the new faces of global Christianity. We do not know what the future will bring, but one thing is abundantly clear: The church that opened the 20th century will look quite different from the church that dominates the 21st century. This emerging church will be far more apostolic, far more supernaturalistic, far more evangelistic, and candidly, far more like the first church than what many of us have known. Prepare to be encouraged. Prepare to be amazed. Most of all, prepare to join in this great global expanse of the gospel!

—Timothy C. Tennent, PhD
President, Professor of World Christianity,
Asbury Theological Seminary

THE WHOLE GOSPEL FOR THE WHOLE WORLD

"The astonishing religious changes of the twentieth century have produced a post-Christian West and a post-Western Christianity."
–Andrew F. Walls

Over the last century, the face of Christianity has radically changed. As we look at the world around us today we find that the church is growing at an explosive rate in many parts of the majority world. As historian Phillip Jenkins has noted, since the beginning of the 20th century, the center of gravity of Christianity has shifted south and east, to Africa, Asia, and Latin America.[1] The growth of global Christianity is intimately tied to church planting movements that have crossed cultural, language, and geographic boundaries, proliferating around the world.[2] To better understand this phenomenon, consider the following statistics: In 1910, about two-thirds of the world's Christians lived in Europe, where the bulk of Christians had been for a millennium. Today, about one in four Christians live in sub-Saharan Africa (24 percent), and about one in eight are found in Asia and the Pacific (13 percent). The number of Christians around the world has nearly quadrupled in the last 100 years, from about 600 million in 1910 to more than 2 billion in 2010. More than 1.3 billion Christians live in the Global South (61 percent), compared with about 860 million in the Global North (39 percent).[3]

There is a lot we can learn from the global church by looking at what God is doing through these movements. Because of the growth of Global Christianity, the flow of evangelism has reversed from the recent past. Gone are the days where people regarded mission as flowing "from the West to the rest."[4] In recent days, the churches of the Majority World have undertaken the task of re-evangelizing the Western world with the gospel of Jesus Christ. The 21st century gave rise to over 420,000 missionaries, only 12-15 percent of whom were from the West.[5] British author Martin Robinson speaks of these missionaries who are now coming to the West from nations like Brazil, Haiti, Mexico, Nigeria, Dominican Republic, and Ethiopia, just to name a few.[6] With such a global presence, there is a lot that we can learn from our brothers and sisters in the wider global church who are scattered throughout the world. We live in a truly global and multicultural world, where Christian leaders must be missionally minded and globally engaged. As John Stott suggested, "We must be global Christians with a global vision because our God is a global God."[7]

THE WHOLE BIBLE FOR THE WHOLE WORLD

The mission of Christ was at the heart of why Asbury Theological Seminary was founded. The founders impressed upon the identity of our school a simple vision to bring the "Whole Bible for the Whole World." Since its inception in 1923, the seminary has grown to become a truly globally engaged theological institution in the United States with a recent average of over 1,700 members of the student body, representing more than 90 denominations and 29 countries, plus 10,000 alumni who live in nearly 70 countries. We estimate that in the next 10 years, almost 40 percent of our student body will be trained in global church planting, positioning Asbury Seminary as a global catalyst for new faith communities around the world!

In order to contribute toward the needs of an increasingly multicultural, secular, and global context for mission, Asbury Seminary launched the Church Planting Initiative in 2015 to help equip church leaders to plant new churches and to revitalize existing congregations so they can become reproducing disciple-making movements. Since that time, we have developed a variety of training opportunities such as a Master of Arts degree in Intercultural Studies with an emphasis in church planting and a non-academic church-planting institute for church leaders around the world to equip them to fulfill the Great Commission as they live out the *missio Dei* in their local context of ministry. While we want to offer resources as we train those around the world, we are also committed to learning from the global church. This is the missionary way, as it were. Our goal in having a two-way learning environment in this way is to mutually share what we're learning from those with boots on the ground to other practitioners and students who are committed to reproducing disciple-making disciples of Jesus Christ around the world.

This book is an effort to take what we've learned not just from the classroom but also from boots on the ground and share it with a broader audience. The eight stories that comprise this book come from our Global Church Planting Summit in June of 2017 with more than 60 church planters representing mission in 20 countries. It was called the CPI Global Summit, sponsored by Asbury's Church Planting Initiative. We gathered together for four days in Manchester, England, to hear stories of God's faithfulness around the world in the form of case studies and other formats. These case studies, keynote presentations, testimonies, and devotional talks provided first-hand reports of the Spirit raising up new faith communities. What we shared together was so powerful and helpful, we had to compile it for those who were not in attendance. That's this book. The rich conversations and all that we witnessed during this gathering infused us with awe and wonder; we hope that those stories, as retold in written format, will elicit the same in you.

Whether it was establishing schools in Muslim areas or starting suicide care groups in a highly secularized society, our gathering carried with it as many planting models as we had people in attendance. The case studies included snapshots of God's activity to reach the lost from fields in countries like Jerusalem, India, Canada, the UK, Columbia, China, Kenya and New Zealand. The Summit fostered a learning environment through deep friendships and vital networking. The words of Dr. Gregg Okesson, Dean of the E. Stanley Jones School of World Mission and Evangelism, capture well the spirit of the event:

The Global Summit offered a fantastic opportunity to learn collaboratively with global leaders in church planting. The case study approach facilitated the cross-fertilization of learning. The Summit, likewise, led to new friendships around the world. For me, the Summit has been one of the highlights of my time at Asbury! We are continuing to learn from the experiences we heard from our brothers and sisters around the world and are excited to incorporate these lessons into the way we view church planting at Asbury.

THE CASE-STUDY APPROACH

The relationships formed and the content shared at the Global Summit were too good for us not to share it with the rest of the world. This book that you are about to read is the fruit of the 2017 Global Church Planting Summit in Manchester, England, that I mentioned above. It contains eight case studies from some of our global presenters. The following case studies are about the uniqueness of church planting in various local contexts, representing a variety of global perspectives on mission. The goal of sharing these case studies is to help us better understand the context in which God has placed us. It is our hope that this book will paint a picture of the diversity of global church planting, as well as inspire reflection, conversation, and collaboration. I like to think of the global church as a multi-colored mosaic: each fragment displays a different hue, but in unison, these individual pieces portray a beautiful masterpiece. Today, many different expressions and types of church plants exist as part of the body of Christ. We celebrate those and what God has done through them, even as we learn from them.

Rather than simply telling what is happening in global church planting, we have taken a case-study approach that introduces readers to the diversity of global church planting from a variety of specific real-life contexts in their own words. A case study is designed to offer an in-depth investigation of a distinct people group or community using data that is gathered from a variety of sources that often includes observations and interviews. In this book, the case studies are first-hand accounts from church planting leaders in their own words about their particular global context. Each chapter features a case study from around the globe that reminds us we need new local churches to reach all types of people for Christ in each global context. Our contributors are expert practitioners faithfully living out the great commission in their cultural context. Their stories and insights offer valuable lessons for those of us who want to learn more about what God is doing in and through the global church.

The final section contains an epilogue from Dr. Gregg Okesson, Dean of the School of World Missions at Asbury Seminary, who offers his reflections on the case studies. In the appendices, Dr. Jay Moon, Professor of Evangelism and Church Planting at Asbury Seminary, has written a study guide that goes with each chapter with questions that can be used for either personal reflection or group discussion. Finally, at the end, the Appendix called, "Struggles and Lessons from Global Church Planters," contains content from interviews with global church planters that provides valuable insight into both the struggles that church planters face and the lessons they have learned that promote health and spiritual vitality.

In closing, this book can be used in a number of ways. It can be read individually and in a group setting; it can be used in seminary and Bible college classrooms; and it can be used by as they guide students and practitioners through issues related to global church planting and mission. You can also access other helpful resources and case studies at our website www.asburychurchplanting.com. Whoever you are and wherever you serve—whether you're a missionary on the back streets of Beijing, China, or a missional leader in the suburbs of Houston, Texas—we pray this resource will help you as you join in God's mission.

—Dr. Winfield Bevins,
Director of Church Planting,
Asbury Theological Seminary

CHRISTIAN MOBILIZATION IN MEDELLÍN

Free Methodist Church Planting Movement, Colombia

B. Elizabeth Gómez and
Rev. Ricardo Gómez, Ph.D.

Claudia and Gustavo were struggling financially and their marriage was crumbling. They had stopped going to church a while back, and their thirteen-year-old son was trapped in watching pornography. They started attending small group meetings at a neighbor's apartment. Thanks to the challenges of that group and the pastoral counseling they received, they have experienced deep healing. Their marriage improved, Gustavo gained a steady job, and they were able to dedicate more time to their son. Claudia started helping lead a group of abused women and their home has become a place of refuge for their friends and family. In fact, in March 2017 Gustavo and Claudia began leading an Alpha Course[1] in their home for a group of their son's friends.

Fabián had smoked *basuco*[2] for over thirty years when his boss started having "motivational" meetings at the factory. Even in his altered state, what the leader was saying made sense to him, and he decided to stop his daily use of the drug, though he occasionally caves to the temptation. His coworkers and family noticed the change in him, and rather than simply waiting for his next hit, he started dreaming of serving God in the church and helping others flee from drug addiction and providing job training for them.

Ten-year-old Julian's father was a drug dealer. Despite living in a home of physical abuse, Julian was smart and dreamed of becoming a medical doctor. When the church started hosting a kids' club in the community center, Julian always attended. In 2015, they gave him a book called *The Story*.[3] The book was so interesting to him that he took it to school and read it during recess. A few weeks later, Julian went back to kids' club and asked for an extra book. He said his teacher wanted to know what he was reading. Julian had the pleasure of presenting him with a book and also leading his teacher to Christ.

For as long as anyone could remember, Maria had been the neighborhood drunk. She never learned to read or write and had never married. Cleaning homes and drinking every night were the routines of this sixty-year-old woman's existence. If someone insulted her beloved professional soccer team, it would incite her anger and lead to some very ugly fights. But suddenly, almost overnight, Maria changed. A woman named Amparo befriended her and invited her to a meeting in her home. Maria accepted the invitation, and it was there that she learned about a personal relationship with Jesus and asked him into her heart. From that night forward, she stopped drinking alcohol and was baptized in the *Camino de Vida* church one year later. She faithfully attends small group meetings and arrives early to church every week. Though she can't read the Bible, she practically memorizes every lesson and sermon and shares what she has learned with her friends. Not only is Maria spreading God's Word but she is also encouraging many others in their faith due to the transformative work of God in her life.

BACKGROUND AND CONTEXT

It's stories like these that represent God's deep transformative work that has swelled in Medellín, the second largest city in Colombia.[4] Medellín was named the Most Innovative City in the world[5] in 2013, and although God is at work in the lives of the people, there is still a lot of work to be done (despite the innovations that have transformed aspects of society). Gangs still rule many of Medellín's streets, and the city remains the drug capital of Colombia.[6]

While it is reported that 92 percent of Colombians profess to be Christian,[7] little transformation happens beyond the celebration of religious holidays and long-held traditions. Syncretism[8] has marked society with split-level Christianity[9] that reduces the gospel to rituals and traditions. Liberation theology[10] grew out of Catholicism, the official religion of Colombia until 1991,[11] to address the rampant societal needs of poverty and oppression, but it was eventually linked to communism and became revolutionary. Despite this, there is evidence of positive transformation within the church, particularly since Vatican II, which put the Bible into the hands of the people and allowed Mass to be administered in the language of the people. The more recent innovation of holding Sunday Mass in Medellín's shopping malls provides neutral places for the church to reconnect with the populace.

Pentecostals are the largest group of Protestants in Colombia and the most rapidly growing. While their numbers increase, their dispensationalist[12] teachings and the prosperity gospel[13] that many of them espouse have created a dualistic world-view and damaged Christian credibility.

Although the Catholic and Protestant churches have recently united to address specific political concerns,[14] their combined influence on issues facing Medellín residents has been minimal thereby demonstrating their poor theology and nominalism.[15]

Into this context, the Free Methodist Church felt the Holy Spirit's leading to begin a movement of church planting in the city of Medellín. This fits into the strategic goals of the denomination to "fuel and sustain a biblical movement to reach Latin Americans for Christ" by:

1. Empowering and coaching national leaders to multiply disciples, groups, leaders, and churches.
2. Catalyzing initiatives and partnerships to plant clusters of churches in strategic cities.
3. Creating appropriate structures and sustainable systems to encourage and support the exponential growth of the church.[16]

The testimonies of God's work in the lives of Claudia, Gustavo, Fabían, Julian, and Maria—their stories above—are some of the fruit of this young movement.

STRUCTURE AND STRATEGY

Empowering Local Leaders for Multiplication

The Rev. Dr. Ricardo Gómez[17] and his wife, Beth, were assigned to Medellín as missionaries through Free Methodist World Missions (FMWM) in 2013. The Gómezes had previously served the organization by planting an urban church in the city of Santiago, Chile (2009-2012). Their first priority in Medellín was to find a group of leaders to create a strategic team for church planting.

John Jairo Leal[18] and his wife, Susana Castro,[19] pastored an independent church located in *Comuna 5*,[20] one of the areas with the highest levels of gang activity and prostitution in the city. After much research and necessary process, their independent church became a Free Methodist church with a new name, *Comunidad Cristiana Camino de Vida* (Christian Community Walk of Life). The Leal-Castros joined the Gómezes in 2014 to make their church the base from which new churches would be planted.

Rossemberg Patiño[21] was a member and leader of the Free Methodist Church in Barrancabermeja, Colombia. He received a scholarship from the denomination and moved to Medellín in 2014 to study at the FUSBC as well as be mentored by the Gómezes and work alongside them in the church-planting project.

Luis Fernando Perez,[22] originally from Bogotá, moved to Medellín to attend the FUSBC (Bachelors in Theology, 2014), where he met his wife, Astrid Martinez, the seminary librarian. They had served as youth pastors and small group leaders in another denomination but left over ecclesiological issues and joined *Camino de Vida*. He was invited to join the church-planting team in 2015.

Juan Ricardo Castrillon[23] and his wife, Catalina Herrera, joined the team in January 2017 as they began a new ministry in the city because they desired pastoral care and mentoring. Castrillon, a former Wesleyan pastor, is currently the academic dean at *Cristo Para Las Naciones* (Christ for the Nations - CPN).

Catalyzing Initiatives and Partnerships for Clusters of Churches

When the Latin American leadership team chose to adopt the Community Church Planting model (CCP)[24] to plant churches throughout the continent, the Leal-Castros along with some of the key leaders in their church had already completed CCP training through one of the training center platforms and had already begun teaching it to the leadership team. The CCP model, developed by Dr. Bruce Bennett, has the goal of populating all communities with spiritually mature churches. Bennett says this will happen when disciples are multiplying disciples, pastors are multiplying pastors, and churches are multiplying churches—all of which clearly aligns with the Free Methodist goals.

The CCP model embraces different platforms from which to launch new churches, and the church planting team in Medellín is utilizing all of them to some degree. Every church exists within a context. Since each neighborhood is different and every leader is different, no two churches are alike even though they may contain similar elements. Their launching platforms must reflect those differences as well:

A. MOBILIZING CHURCH MEMBERS

Camino de Vida is employing a church-based platform of the CCP model. The church structure includes Integral Growth Groups. These groups make new disciples and develop new leaders. As of 2017, thirty small groups meet in homes throughout the city, ministering to 150 new people in addition to the church's 170 members. Leal and Castro understand that planting new churches oxygenates the parent church, thus making more space for new people.

To prepare for such growth, the church offers weekly training and discipleship for the group leaders. The leader of each group must mentor an apprentice who learns to exercise their leadership skills within the group. As new groups form, the apprentice becomes the group leader and starts training their own apprentice. All groups are volunteer-led and meet in individual homes, providing multiplication with minimum expense.

Integral Growth Group #1. *Aranjuez* is a low-income neighborhood located across the Medellín River from the neighborhood where *Camino de Vida* was originally located.[25] It is a vulnerable area with a very distinct culture because the majority of its residents were internally displaced from coastal Colombia due to either work or violence.[26]

Juan Diego, an eight-year-old from that neighborhood, attended a church outreach event and the thirteen-week *"Gran Aventura"* discipleship resource for follow-up that was sponsored by Samaritan's Purse in 2013. He wanted all of his friends to learn what he had learned, and so Liliana Jaramillo was sent to begin a kids' club in *Aranjuez*.

Working through cultural differences, she developed relationships with the children's parents and started a group for adults in 2015. One of the members, Juliana, was baptized and began leading a youth group in 2017. Today, approximately forty people participate in the three groups.

Although the size of the group and its distance from the church make it a viable candidate for becoming its own church, it remains under the umbrella of *Camino de Vida*. The people have been unwilling to take the final step of faith, and Jaramillo has had difficulty developing leaders. Leal says the next step is to send a new leader to work alongside Jaramillo until they can make the healthy transition of leadership and plant a spiritually deep, self-sufficient church.

Integral Growth Group #2. The newest integral growth group is located in *La Esperanza* neighborhood. This is also a low-income neighborhood. It is a more traditional, self-contained Medellín neighborhood, meaning that the same families have lived in it for generations and the neighborhood has little *tiendas* (stores), butcher shops, bakeries, fruit stands, etc., where everyone shops rather than going to the larger supermarkets in other parts of town. Everyone knows everyone in *La Esperanza,* which is why individual transformations are so powerful.

Carlos Rodriguez went through the CCP training with Leal and Castro. He is a very outgoing man and is genuinely concerned for people, making his gift of evangelism particularly effective. A chef by trade, Rodriguez is currently a local ministerial candidate, preparing for ordination within the denomination.

In 2015, Rodriguez opened a pizza parlor near *La Esperanza*. As he began to know the people, he also started sharing Christ with them. His first converts were a single mother and her teenage son. In January 2017, he opened an integral growth group with his two new converts. By April of that year, Rodriguez already had a new leader in training and the group had grown to fifteen participants, all of whom Rodriguez had personally led to Christ.

Rodriguez has the vision, the leadership skills, and the training to officially open a new church in *La Esperanza*. He has proven a desire to continue growing personally, to share Christ and encourage his followers to do the same. While Rodriguez is a valuable leader in the *Camino de Vida* church, Leal and Castro expect that Rodriguez will soon officially become the pastor of a newly formed church in *La Esperanza*.

Center for Family Development. *Camino de Vida* also uses the Center for Family Development (CFD) in the neighborhood *Caribea* as another church planting model. This particular neighborhood is a mixture of low-income and "squatter" homes. To enter the neighborhood, one must literally enter through a haze of *basuco* smoke and with the permission of the gang leaders.

In April 2016, the church asked to use the small two-story community center to offer daily programming to children between the ages of five and eleven. Thanks to church member donations of money, material, and labor, it has been equipped for homework assistance, sports training, and English classes—all led by volunteers. Children are also given a snack every day. Parents are responsible for paying 4,000 pesos (less than a dollar and a quarter USD) per month, but the majority of the ministry is financed through *Camino de Vida* designated giving.

In 2017, Pastor Luz Mery Moscote became the CFD director and started a second-hand store to help finance the ministry. She receives a small offering of about 100 dollars a month from the church-planting budget.[27]

B. MOBILIZING INDIVIDUALS

The second platform for CCP utilized in Medellín is the individual and home-based strategy. The Perez-Martinez family and the Castrillon-Herrera family are both operating under this model.

The Business and Relationship Model. In January 2017, Perez was asked to plant a church in a middle-class portion of the city for which he receives a small salary of about 300 dollars per month from the church-planting budget.

His work base was an integral growth group started by a Camino de Vida member, Marlene, who lives in that area of the city. She asked Perez to visit her nephews, Rodrigo and German, who own and operate a packaging company. The company was experiencing both financial and paranormal difficulties. Everyone who worked there testified to the presence of a ghost that made noises, opened and closed doors, turned on and off lights, and contributed to the already high stress level within the company.

Rodrigo was not religious but, given the situation, he asked Perez to pray for the company. Perez obliged but he wasn't content to make this prayer a one-time deal. He began meeting with Rodrigo on a weekly basis. Rodrigo invited him to lead motivational meetings for his staff that eventually became Bible study meetings. Now Perez is the company chaplain. The business has improved, lives are being transformed, and the ghost has not been heard again.

At the same time, Perez is making connections with people at the public sports complex, one of the central gathering spots of that region of the city. Despite the jokes that Perez goes to the gym to exercise his tongue, he is developing intentional friendships, the first step in evangelism.

His morning workouts have resulted in some significant connections:

1. He was invited to be the spiritual director for a training group. When the trainer moved away, Perez maintained contact with people in the group. He is able to listen to and address the issues in people's lives as he hikes Medellín's mountain trails with them every week.
2. He started a WhatsApp group with five men he met at the gym. The primary purpose of the group is to help one another improve their English skills. As he gains their confidence Perez is able to provide Biblical advice and encouragement.

The key to this method of church planting is developing and maintaining strong, loyal relationships. The challenge, particularly within this sector of society, is that people do not realize their need for God and have developed a set of reasons not to believe in God. Others just lack the courage to take a step of faith and believe in him fully. While the slow pace sometimes frustrates him, particularly knowing God's transformative power that is available, Perez understands that building true and lasting community takes time. He says that the timeline is lengthened in Medellín based upon its history of conflict: "People are slow to trust, they are slow to commit, and they've lost confidence in the church due to the poor testimony of its leaders."

The Insider Advantage. Closed-gate neighborhoods and apartment complexes in Medellín are most common in middle- and upper-class neighborhoods. Castrillon and Herrera felt called to minister to this unreached people group. They moved into one such neighborhood and began inviting friends and neighbors to meet in their home, creating a Christian movement for the transformation of the city called *Movimiento Renovación* (Renovation Movement). Their meetings contain the traditional elements of a church service along with specific challenges to live according the week's Biblical teachings.

Their small living room was quickly filled with about twenty-five to thirty people of all ages, and they began to train Alpha Course leaders to start groups in their own homes. In March 2017, they opened three Alpha groups and the results have been good, though not what Castrillon and Herrera expected because:

1. The way Alpha is designed makes the process a little slower than they expected
2. Several of the people who attend groups are already members of, though not attending, other churches.

This means that the process of renewal in them is to provide them the healing they need and then return them to their church.

Castrillon says that before beginning more Alpha groups they will provide better leader training and hold an "open" event in each neighborhood where the course will be offered. This will allow the church to serve the neighborhood and enable the neighborhood to get to know the hosts. In addition to Alpha groups, Herrera is ministering to women in a lower income neighborhood of the city. Castrillon and Herrera hope to open a CFD in the same neighborhood. This is one of the benefits of working as a team: *Movimiento Renovación* and *Camino de Vida* are learning from one another.

C. MOBILIZING SEMINARY STUDENTS

The seminary-based CCP platform is also being employed in Medellín. This is the platform in which seminaries provide practical church planting training and then send out their graduates to practice and train others. Patiño is actually implementing a combination of this model and the church platform model. He fulfills his ministry-based practicum through service to the *Camino de Vida* church. After he completed the church-planting course taught by R. Gómez at the seminary, he was sent to lead an integral growth group in a neighborhood called *Robledo Pelicanos*.

Establishing Christian Gangs. *Robledo Pelicanos* is a low-class neighborhood on the periphery of the city consisting of three apartment complexes with approximately five-hundred individual apartments in each. Gangs have established invisible borders between each complex, restricting the free movement of people from one complex to another. For this reason, the group's influence is currently limited to one complex.

Perez started this group in May 2016, when a friend moved into the neighborhood. He went door to door inviting people to participate in a small group. Children were interested but few adults. He befriended one man named Alberto but only ever visited with him from the doorway because Alberto's wife, Carmen, was a staunch Catholic and was very prejudiced against Protestants.

When Alberto died Perez took a basket of food to Carmen and her two children. She was so touched that she asked Perez to begin a group in her apartment. She said, "I am Catholic and I'm not going to change, but I'd like to hear what you have to say." That's when Perez invited Patiño to join him. Carmen, her adult daughter, and a few other women showered them with questions each week like, "What do you think about Mary and the saints? Why do you pray differently?" Rather than fight about faith and make enemies, Perez and Patiño listened and answered questions, building upon the similarities of the Catholic and Protestant traditions rather than the differences.

Martinez began a club for children that met in a small, enclosed room that had once been used to house the complex garbage. By the time Patiño began working with the Perez-Martinezes, there were nine children in the group.

When Perez was sent to plant a church in the south, Patiño took over the group leadership. He invited a fellow seminary student and *Camino de Vida* member, Andres Restrepo, to work with him. They continued to meet weekly with the group of adult women, one of whom offered her home for the children's meetings. Sixteen children attended the first meeting in her home. By mid-March, there were twenty-five children of all ages attending the weekly meetings, and the team decided to begin a group for teens.

One mother asked Patiño to help her thirteen-year-old daughter, Tatiana. She said, "I'd rather see my daughter pregnant than doing drugs." Although the mother doesn't attend the adult group he leads, she agreed to host the youth meetings. Twelve teenagers attended the first meeting and by the beginning of May, there were thirty-eight children (ages five to eleven) and teens (ages thirteen to seventeen) regularly attending the weekly meetings.

Patiño and Restrepo receive a small offering from *Camino de Vida* to cover their transportation to and from the neighborhood. Both the church-planting team and the church leadership agree that *Robledo Pelicanos* should be an autonomous church plant, following the CFD model since they primarily work with children and women at this time. They agree that they need a more neutral meeting place so that people from the other apartment complexes can attend. However, gang activity significantly increased just as they began looking for a place to rent. The gangs established a 6:00 p.m. curfew for children and began heavy recruitment of children and teenagers. In the first two weeks of May 2017, four children from the neighborhood were reported missing: two were found alive but two little girls were found, having been raped and killed.

While the gang activity has halted the search for a church location, the ministry continues. Patiño says that the existence of the church in this neighborhood is particularly important because of the constant danger imposed upon children and teens by the gangs: "We are presenting a distinct alternative to what the world around them is continually offering. As we walk with them, we are encouraged because we see that not only are they learning but their behaviors are changing." He concluded, "God is at work in this place."

In June, during Colombian school vacations, Restrepo arrived to lead the youth group only to find that Tatiana and her family weren't home. One of the other youths asked his older brother if they could meet in his home. Not only did Brayen grant his permission but also participated in the group meeting. At the end, he pulled Restrepo aside and said, "What you are doing here is good. We need a church in this neighborhood and so here is some money to help rent or buy a place to hold it." Restrepo told him that before he could accept the money, he'd like Brayen to meet with Pastor Leal. The next day, Brayen attended Camino de Vida church and met with Leal. He has been attending leadership training meetings and hosting a group of his young adult friends and faithfully giving to the church-planting project ever since.

The church-planting team knows that God is in complete control of this movement. He is equipping different people to serve different neighborhoods and sectors of society. The role of the team is to help each leader and church live up to the vision that God has given them. They are careful to ensure that the structures and systems they adopt will serve the mission of God and not vice versa. They need to ensure that these structures do not cripple the growth of the church but rather enable it.

Structures and Systems to Support the Growth of the Church

The Free Methodist Church Planting Movement is, at the time of this writing, still a very young movement, but the Holy Spirit is leading it. He is putting leaders and other people together to bring about deep and lasting transformation in the city of Medellín, Colombia. As he calls his followers to be good stewards of what he gives them, the church-planting team has developed a few key structures to sustain the movement.

The most important component of this structure is the pastoral care group. Each week the pastors share and evaluate one another's ministry plans and results. In their meetings, they share their visions, provide support to one another, and hold one another accountable. As they encounter challenges and problems in both the ministry and the personal lives of the leaders, they work together as a team toward a resolution. They avoid the temptation to impatiently pressure leaders for results and instead seek God's wisdom to know when to provide encouragement and applause and when to provide an extra push.

As churches multiply, leaders are also multiplying. Currently, *Camino de Vida* relies upon more than sixty leaders for the expansion of the kingdom of God in Medellín. Likewise, *Movimiento Renovación* is training and sending out people to open Alpha Courses in their own closed-gate neighborhoods, where traditional churches cannot enter. The challenge is ensuring that the leaders are well-trained and discipled so that they can successfully continue to reproduce biblically sound leaders. Pastoral care groups are key in ensuring this. Each leader not only attends a pastoral care group of their own but also leads one for the men and women they have trained.

CHALLENGES

Challenges of Context

The church-planting team firmly believes that the resources required for church growth come in the harvest itself as seen in the case of Brayen. However, they are challenged by the fact that many of the churches they are starting are in low-income neighborhoods or minister primarily to children. To address this reality, the Colombian church-planting budget committee has agreed to provide support on a decreasing scale for five years. In year one and year two, the church plant receives 100 percent of the agreed upon financial support. As the church establishes, that support decreases to 75 percent in year three, 50 percent in year four, and 25 percent in the fifth year. By the sixth year, the denomination expects the church to be fully self-supporting. Groups like the CFD are also exploring and exercising creative ways to fund their ministries.

Financial Challenges

Of course, this leads to another challenge within the Free Methodist group: the fear of asking for money. The damage caused by prosperity gospel teachings that enriched church leaders is widespread in Medellín. As a result, the general population tends to be suspicious of any mention of money, and pastors are afraid to teach about biblical stewardship. To combat this, both Leal and Castrillon have invited Ricardo Gómez to teach and challenge their churches or groups on this subject.

Structures of Access

Another challenge to planting churches in Medellín is developing structures to actually gain access to the people. This requires creativity. In *Robledo Pelicanos*, it involved the hard work of going door-to-door and the danger of crossing invisible borders. *Camino de Vida's* Center for Family Development had to establish a non-threatening presence in the neighborhood, and *Movimiento Renovación* has to gain access to closed-gate neighborhoods, a task requiring the true incarnation of living among the people. No matter what method is used, they all require the patience of intentionally establishing purposeful relationships.

CONCLUSION

The Free Methodist Church has started a movement of church planting in Medellín, Colombia. It is a movement that reflects the diversity of the city itself. This case study reflects the initial stages of this church-planting movement using the CCP model as its base to multiply leaders, pastors, and churches. This reflects the Free Methodist mission and vision in Latin America.

The case study described some of the transformation that God is doing in Colombia's second largest city. Rather than planting one church, God has put together a team of leaders in Medellín to start a church-planting movement to start numerous churches based upon various methods described in CCP. These include mobilizing church members, mobilizing individuals and groups, and mobilizing seminary students. As the case study demonstrates, it is a fluid movement with varying degrees of success.

No one knows what the future holds, and the team realizes that it still has a lot to learn. Nevertheless, the Free Methodist church-planting team in Medellín believes that God is the Lord of the Harvest and that he is in control. They advance according to his strength and wisdom rather than their own. They know that God is capable of much deeper transformation in the city of Medellín and are honored to be a part of it.

KENYA'S URBAN CHALLENGE

Good Shepherd Africa Gospel Church, Nairobi

Patrick L. Murunga

The church in Africa finds itself at a crossroads. Urbanization is taking place at an alarming rate. Various statistics tell us that by 2050 most of the world's population will be living in cities.[1] This phenomenon of urbanization is happening at one of the highest rates in Africa. It is estimated that 50 percent of the population of Africa will live in cities by 2025.[2] Additionally, four of the world's 25 largest cities will be found in Africa by 2025.

The city of Nairobi, for example, began as a "tent city," and it has grown to a modern city complete with skyscrapers, shopping malls, residential districts, factories, parks, social clubs, etc., and is projected to be one of the four largest cities in the world with a population of more than 16 million people.[3] Kenya—the country in which Nairobi dwells—has one of the highest population growth rates in the world: its population doubles every seventeen years.[4] With such a staggering urban growth rate, it is my opinion that the church needs to find ways to minister effectively.

It is apparent that one of the primary reasons that people move into cities is because they hope to find a better life. They hope to find employment and pursue better education and better opportunities in life. Unfortunately, as they settle into the city, their dreams are shattered. The alarming fact is that they arrive poorly prepared for the pressures and realities of city life. They soon discover that the jobs, education, and better life they dreamt about was only a mirage. They find themselves in the city with no job, no education, no better life, and no hope. They are disillusioned and hopeless. As they struggle to eke out a living, they fall into wrong hands and end up in crime and other social ills. For most of them, going back to their rural homes is not an option. Having no place to live, they end up in informal settlements; poor and with no means of sustenance, their situation is dire. They end up in anti-social behavior or join other illegal organizations because they need to survive.

Calling the Church to Action

It's my opinion that the church must help at this point. The church needs to take the initiative to look for these new people and provide them with both spiritual and physical help. Aylward Shorter agrees. He says that the vast majority of new immigrants are poor—up to about 70 percent.[5] Urban poverty offers the church one of its greatest challenges.

I belong to the Africa Gospel Church, Kenya. The denomination is a late entrant in urban work, although it entered Kenya through the work of missionaries of World Gospel Mission in 1932. Most missionary work was concentrated among the rural people in the South Rift of Kenya. To date, because of the work done, the church is 1,800 congregations strong.

Urban work in Nairobi was started on November 15, 1973. Good Shepherd Church, under the leadership of missionary pastors, grew from the initial 6 people in 1973 to over 800 people in 1997. This is a multi-ethnic, multi-socioeconomic church located on a major highway, some 10 kilometers from downtown Nairobi. From its inception, missionaries from America and Ireland led Good Shepherd Church. The last of the missionaries left in 1997. Today, Good Shepherd Church has grown to about 1,200 members under local leadership.

BEGINNING STAGES

I am a native of Nairobi, having joined the pastoral staff of Good Shepherd Church in 1989. I served for 25 years before retiring to take up other responsibilities within the denomination. When I joined the church, there was no significant effort to plant new churches. Every year the church had as one of its goals, "To firmly plant several new churches in Nairobi and the surrounding areas,"[6] but nothing was done. Along with others in the church, I decided to make this goal a reality.

In preparation to plant a new congregation, we did a lot of reading and research on the growth and health of the church in Nairobi. A report based on research conducted by a team from Daystar University in Nairobi in 1989 emerged that indicated, "The church was growing at five percent, while the population growth was at seven percent per year."[7] Niemeyer, the lead researcher, observed that only 11.3 percent of the population attended church on any given Sunday. This figure includes all churches, regardless of their affiliation, in the city. The report emphasized that a very small number of the churches were evangelical. It was discovered further that about 6 out of 100 people were in an evangelical church on a given Sunday. The number of those who would not be in a gospel-preaching church was 74 percent.

The report shows that many regions within the city of Nairobi desperately need churches. Some regions have one church for every 442 people, but in other regions, there is only one church for 15,000 people. In 1985, there were about 900 churches, with roughly 40 new church plants each year. According to my calculations, just to keep up with the population growth, the number of church plants must be increased more than threefold with at least 200 people in each one of them. These statistics tug at the heart of the leadership of the Good Shepherd Church. The leadership of our church realized that if the church were to live up to its vision for reaching the city for Christ, we would need to wake up now and get on with this vision.

The local church council, in a 1990s meeting, gave its blessing for the pastoral team to assemble a church-planting team to go ahead and plant its first daughter church. Since my wife and I had been keen on church planting, I asked to help with this first church plant. The local church council agreed to allow my involvement. Under the leadership of the then Senior Pastor, John Muehleisen, a team was assembled. They quickly realized that it was not enough to know about the needy and lost people, or even to have a strategy and finances to plant a church, unless the right personnel had been identified and trained for effective church planting. Therefore, the first thing that the pastoral team at Good Shepherd Church did was to select the church-planting team.[8]

About clarification of the leadership of the new church, it was agreed that the church-planting team would serve as the board of the new church. On a traditional board, many of the board members are not necessarily active in ministry but serve mostly as the ones who check on and make sure policies are implemented. In the new church, though, every board member was equal and expected to give input and direction to the church. Because of his position as chairman, the pastor had more responsibilities than the others to make sure that everything was running smoothly.

The team met weekly for the next year. Time was spent in prayer, Bible study, training, and bonding. The team also seriously canvassed the city for possible sites for the new church plant. Within about six months of its existence, the church-planting team unanimously felt led by the Lord to plant a daughter church in Mugoya, South C. As captured in an undated minute by Sarah Weiss, "Mugoya Estate is where God seems to have called us the church-planting team from Good Shepherd Church to build a church and minister to the people there."[9] Mugoya Estate at the time was one of the fastest growing regions of the city. It is a mainly middle to upper class residential estate.

The team was then asked to ensure that a core team of Christians in the targeted area were identified and recruited. These would be people who would act as gate openers for the church-planting team into their estate.[10] These people, together with the church-planting team, formed the core team. By this time, the church-planting team had worked on a philosophy, vision, mission, and organization of the church, and assigned responsibilities to team members.

STRATEGY AND STRUCTURE

The church-planting team decided that in obedience to Christ's command as contained in his final words of Matthew 28, "Therefore, go and make disciples of all nations…" the church plant would share Christ's message with *all* who do not know Christ. For this reason, members of the team would share the gospel with a clear intention of leading the hearers to make an informed decision for Christ. Furthermore, the team desired to help new believers grow and become active members of the church.

What's more, the team decided that it was its goal to not only be content in planting this single church but also that the leadership would make its reason for existence the planting of other daughter churches. However, this would be achieved by collaborating with the mother church, as well as other likeminded local churches in Nairobi and beyond.

How We Developed Our Plan

When the new church plant, Good News, started, the leadership deliberately took steps to be intentional in connecting with one another and connecting with the community. Having studied the Book of Acts together, the team connected regularly through a time of prayer, worship, and fellowship. Indeed, just like the church in Acts, the leadership of Good News Church had spent considerable time in prayer because they felt the leading of God to start the church as the apostles did in Acts 1:12-14—through prayer.

The team further observed that in the book of Acts those gathered in the upper room were believers from the four corners of the world, and they felt that the new fellowship would need to embrace people from all levels of society even though the location of the church was in an upper middle-class neighborhood. In the book of Acts the Holy Spirit made this fact obvious, that the church God was creating was not to cater to one ethnic group. He strongly overruled any intentions the disciples might have had that the church would be Jewish (Acts 2:5, 8-10).

The team also observed from Acts that the driving vision of the early church was to live out a life of radical Christian discipleship and fellowship. The early leadership of Good News believed the practice of the disciples in Acts was meant to guide the community of this brand-new church in every area of life. That true Christian living shows forth the fruits of radical discipleship and fellowship: open and loving relationships, full sharing of material resources, a visible common life, active witness for justice and peace, and a priority on living out the Word of the Lord rather than talking about it (Acts 2:44-47). Reasoning this way led the church to formulate and adopt as its motto: "Good News Africa Gospel Church is a loving, caring, and sharing fellowship."

The pulpit ministry was another area of focus. In Acts, we see real people taking seriously the command of Jesus to win others to Christ through powerful preaching. Here we see the young dynamic church at its best. Though forbidden to preach the gospel of Jesus Christ, they were not intimidated. They made it clear that they intended to keep preaching the clear message of salvation through the risen Christ. The leadership of the church plant latched on to this. Preaching in the church would therefore be Christ-centered, as seen in Acts 2:22-23. The pulpit would be the place where the message of salvation would be preached clearly, and it would be a place from which we would ask for a response from the listeners, as seen in Acts 2:37-40.

We took our plan from the early church, but we needed a practical plan, too. That's where mapping our target location came in.

Mapping the Target Location

Choosing the location of a church plant is very important. Here's how the rubber hit the road for us as we embarked on finding the location of our church. Our team observed that bungalows and mansions with modern apartments were rapidly coming up near an area called "Mugoya South C." A drive-in outdoor movie theater was nearby, along with several bars in and around Mugoya.

We noticed a variety of activities and institutions in the area, too, which attracted us. For example, there is a Criminal Investigation Department (CID) training school in the vicinity, a sports facility, and the Ministry of Works (MOW) Sports Club, which is the most popular sports facility in the neighborhood. We found several educational facilities in the neighborhood, as well: a primary school and a new nursery school, too. In fact, our team contacted the owner of the nursery school, Mr. Moses Kamau, who was willing to allow us to start meeting as a church at his premises once their building was completed. We noticed several places of worship in the area, but they were different than what we were planning to do. There were other churches, but the church closest to where we wanted to plant was not evangelical; hence the desperate need to plant a Bible-believing and Bible-teaching church in the neighborhood.

The team prayed hard that God would provide a large enough worship space for the launch. God answered our request and provided a perfect space at the Bellevue Nursery School with very affordable rent. This was indeed a blessing. Having blitzed the place with flyers, door-to-door evangelism, the special events initiated to draw the community into the church, and extensive advertisement announcing the public launch of the new church, we were ready to have a church service.

Our leadership team requested the mother church, on that first Sunday of May 1990, to shift its service to the new church-plant site for the launch. The main speaker was the senior pastor of Good Shepherd Church, Rev. John Muehleisen. While not as many people from the mother church were able to make it, God showed up and we had a total of 150 people in attendance. The lesson we learned on that day was this: Jesus builds his church. No manner of machination, he will bring people to his church. The body of Christ has the responsibility of making known the claims of Christ, and it is his responsibility to bring the people into the church.

OUR INTERNAL STRATEGY AND PLAN

The mother church had agreed to continue its supervisory and support role over the daughter church for a period of five years. The main reason for this was basically to provide a financial covering. The church did not have land of its own, and the plan had been that Good Shepherd Church would assist in the acquisition of potential land. The mother church pledged to give the daughter church a month's support to go toward the pastor's salary.

As stated above, the team met on a weekly basis for prayer, planning, and preparing, making sure that all meetings, except when the team needed to be on site, happened at a team member's house. Meetings were not just for business but also for building relationships through retreats, barbecues, social events, etc. Briefly, the team partied, sweated, took risks, and made memories together.

Praying Together, Giving, and Tithing

The team took prayer very seriously. Right from the beginning, the pastoral team made sure that the church got involved in prayer for the church plant. Even the church-planting team was selected through prayer, and that's why they made prayer one of our key pillars.

Once they were "on the ground," they would spend time walking around the neighborhood praying. On one such prayer walk, the team was shown a house many believed to be that of a witchdoctor, so they prayed like never before. They knew that if they were to have success in this place, God had to intervene and cleanse it. How did it happen? God did it in the form of the Kenyan Government. Eventually, the witchdoctor was evicted from the neighborhood.

The church-planting team, at its inception, felt the need to stop giving its offerings and tithes to the mother church and be released to give directly to the church-planting team's needs. The team believed that doing this right from the beginning would give it a sense of ownership and help it take charge of the affairs of the new church right from the beginning.

By the time of the church's official launch a year later, the team had managed to pay for most of its expenses. By the time of starting, this new church had saved a significant amount of money that would enable it to begin its future work without much assistance from the mother church.

Assigning Roles and Responsibilities

The members of the church-planting team were each assigned a special role and given specific responsibilities. On the team, there was a chairman who was the face of the church-planting team. The chairman had the responsibility of making sure members of the team executed their responsibilities. He called and chaired all the church-planting meetings and mobilized volunteers by assigning them work.

The challenge that the team faced was that there were three different people in very active leadership roles within this new church. Constitutionally, the chairman of any church in the Africa Gospel Church is the pastor. But because the church plant had not officially started, and I had not been officially released to join the new church plant other than merely to offer help, the team leadership gravitated between the lead church-planting trainer, the pastor on the team, and the other gentleman on the team. This was eventually clarified when the church officially started (the following year) and I was officially released to take over as lead pastor.

The second important position to fill was that of the chairman of evangelism. For a church plant, it is very important to evangelize and bring people into the church. The chairman's responsibility was to mobilize the team to go out for evangelism, build relationships, and invite people to church, generally creating opportunities for evangelism in the area.

Another important leadership position was that of the pastor. The team felt that the church would not go far without a duly appointed and installed lead pastor. Whereas evangelism was winning people to Christ and bringing them into the church, the lead pastor was to feed, nurture, and care for the spiritual needs of those who come into the church. The pastor was charged with helping individuals discover their spiritual gifts and talents, as well as encouraging them to use those gifts within the church setting.

Nahum Mensah Jr. was very good when it came to administrative matters. He followed up on all administrative matters: he wrote to everyone with whom the team came into contact while doing evangelism; he responded to inquiries about the church plant; he wrote letters of invitation to possible members; and he and the secretary of the team made sure to take care of all secretarial and financial matters.

Last, but not least, was the position of the worship director. As the team prepared to launch the church, it was important that a worship director be identified and given responsibility to prepare the Sunday worship service, along with the midweek Bible studies. This person needed to be musically inclined, a meticulous person, and a prayer warrior.

Selecting the Pastor

While I was with the church-planting team, and indeed the vision team, right from the beginning, the truth is that I had not officially been released to the church-planting team during those early days. I was still on the payroll of the mother church and essentially served under the authority and leadership of the mother church.

Yet, as the new church took shape, it became apparent that I could not continue serving at the two churches like I was. After much prayer and consultation with the leadership of the mother church, we agreed that it was best to release me from my full-time responsibilities at Good Shepherd Church so I could serve full time at the new daughter church. Releasing me, however, meant that I had to come up with a salary as the new pastor. Again, with the help of the mother church, it was agreed that the mother church would participate in paying the salary of the pastor. They decided that the new church would pay house rent while the mother church would pay the balance of the salary. This, however, did not work out. I ended up taking a part-time job training pastors with a new outfit known as Bible Training Center for Pastors, as well as leading the new church.

COMMUNITY ENGAGEMENT

Thus far, I've addressed our internal strategy and plans, but a major part of our strategy involved our community engagement.

Door-to-Door Evangelism

After much prayer and scouting, we agreed upon a location for starting the church. Then, our immediate task was to make our presence felt in the neighborhood. We did this through door-to-door evangelism in three phases. The main reason for this was not necessarily to win people to Christ but to make ourselves known in the community.

First, because we wanted to blitz the community, we recruited over twenty individuals to come alongside the evangelism team. The team shared about themselves, Christ, and the incoming church. We shared and left *The Four Spiritual Laws* booklets, along with a brochure with details about who we were and our new church in the community.

Second, we followed up with any person who had received the gift of eternal life during phase one. We wanted these people to grow and find a church home. Our goal in this phase was to invite the people to join the new church if they did not presently have a home church.

The last phase was to challenge those who'd accepted Christ (and us) to open their homes for Bible study. Before starting the church, the team felt that it was important to be in the community. Only then would the church really be seen as belonging to the community. Two people opened their homes to allow our team members to conduct Bible studies with them.

Bar Ministry

As the team visited homes, inviting people to the home Bible studies, our team members frequently noticed one thing: the absence of men in the home. In our team's walk about, we noticed that the area had many bars and taverns. It dawned on us that that indeed was where all the men were. The team prayed about how to reach these men, and we decided to start a bar ministry. So the team visited the bars every Wednesday night, brochures in hand, to share about the church and offer an abridged presentation of the gospel. For those who wanted to talk, the team members would avail themselves for that. Our main goal was to establish relationships and invite interested persons to church.

Our bar ministry *did not bring any men* to the church, but it made the new church known and accepted in the neighborhood. It also turned out that a member of the bar-ministry team had been an alcoholic before becoming a believer. He asked the team to release him from his bar ministry assignment. The leadership duly obliged. In addition to door-to-door evangelism and bar ministry, we had several other efforts that are worth mentioning:

- **Saturday Outreach.** Each Saturday for over six months was set aside for outreach to the community through various activities. The activities included, but were not limited to, Saturday Bible club for children, baking and cooking, stitching, and floral arrangement lessons for the women. The men took the lead in organizing barbecues on the street and Saturday socials for the whole family.
- **Children's Ministry.** Children in this neighborhood did not have a place to play other than on the streets. A survey that had been done indicated that the children in this neighborhood were open to being involved in some form of activity outside the home. Since the nursery school had allowed the team to use its facilities, the team organized to have Saturday clubs for the children and Vacation Bible School for them every holiday.
- **Barbecue on the Street.** The team thought this was a crazy idea but did it all the same. The adage, "If you can reach a man's stomach, you can reach his heart" is true. As the people came for free food, the team members took the time to witness to the people and invite them to church. Several men and young people who came to the barbecue started attending the new church as a result of this outreach.
- **Flyer Blitz.** As the team neared its launch date, it decided to blitz the entire area with flyers and brochures, which informed them of the new church in the area. We recruited over forty people from the mother church to help do this. Looking back, this was a good thing. Many from the mother church had never been involved in such a thing. Seeing people respond positively to their invitation, some from the mother church decided to join the new church—to follow up with those they had met and invited to the new church. When the church started the following day, at least thirty people from the community we'd reached the previous day came for the official opening of the church.
- **Baking with the Women.** Women seemed to connect well through the baking lessons we offered, and this made more long-lasting friendships than the activities of the men. Those women who were recruited from this outreach became pillars within the church when it eventually started.

SUCCESSES AND CHALLENGES

A mid-term evaluation uncovered particular strengths as well as particular challenges in our new church. The team, for example, had good working relationships with each other. They also had good training and experience. Most of the team members could carry almost any aspect of the ministry. The team, in its first year of ministry, was creative and open to new ideas. We also made good goals, had knowledge of what needed to be done, and could run a large ministry as a group.

One of our weaknesses, however, which was very evident, was a lack of follow-up, implementing plans, and planning for specifics. This greatly limited our team's effectiveness, and unless we had corrected it, this would have kept the church from growing in quantity and quality.

Overcoming Challenges in Evangelism, Preaching, and Teaching

On the other hand, though, most of the team had good training with regard to evangelism and outreach. As mentioned above, we thought of creative ways to reach the community: brochures, outreach days, bar ministry, home visitation, V.B.S, youth outreach, and inviting people to homes. Wednesdays were set aside for visitations. The team was faithful. Notably, there was an increased participation from those outside the team.

While we had good training, very few people accepted Christ as their personal Savior. Plus, the presentation of the gospel on a personal basis decreased. The number one problem we identified was lack of planning and follow-up. We did not announce or advertise what our team planned. We made few calls on Wednesday nights because our team was not prepared. The team had very good plans, but those "good plans" were not carried out. On top of that, those on the leadership team were not reaching out to bring others to the church.

We were more successful in preaching and teaching, though. The whole team of men participated in the preaching. There was a good attempt by the preaching team to think of the needs of the people and plan ahead—

usually one month in advance and later even three months in advance. The lessons we taught in Sunday school were good for the children, as well. Vacation Bible School was well thought out, planned, and executed. The children gave positive feedback about their first experience of V.B.S.

Yet, we found that there was an over-dependence on two people, those who preached the most throughout the year. The preaching was mostly for the adults, which locked out the youth. The team, at this point in the game, seemed to be losing sight of a core component of one of the initial goals of the church-planting team: training young members for ministry. Interestingly, it was the Senior Pastor of the mother church who caught this. He encouraged the team to coordinate their efforts on this particular item in order that those in attendance would act as participants and not mere spectators.

Overcoming Fellowship and Financial Challenges

We invested a lot of energy to have several social times because African cultures are relational by nature. The team managed to have a good number of people stay after the services to talk. The team's togetherness was very evident, too, because they made time for weekly meetings together. It was observed, however, that while the fellowship among the leaders was deep, the fellowship among the new members of the church and everyone else was often surface-level. Further, there was no structure for the people to meet in small groups to encourage, correct, and use their spiritual gifts on a consistent basis.

With regard to finances, the leadership of the new church intended to have a church that was financially self-supporting within a period of three years. But within one year of its existence, the mother church, which had pledged to give $5,000 per month in contributions to the church, pulled out of that arrangement. Evaluating this gesture, the team realized that all expenses of the church for the first year could have been paid from the team and church offerings. Because of this the church did not miss a step in its ministry to the people of Mugoya. This is excellent and a good model.

As much as the church was able to meet its financial obligations in the first year, though, the danger was that little of the finances were coming from the people of the community; most of the funds were from the leadership team. Another blow to the new church was that they were going to lose the support of three families who had been planning to relocate away from the community of ministry. A lesson we eventually learned was that the team should never have been afraid to ask for money from the people.

Another challenge we faced was how to involve those who were not a part of our team. Those who had been in the church but were not on the official team started taking responsibility in the areas of worship, special songs, prayer, opportunities to share in church, offering, welcoming of visitors, and preparation of the worship center. This was good for our Sunday-morning gatherings, but the team needed to purposefully begin preparing others to take up more significant roles within the leadership of the service and involve them in ministry other than Sunday services only.

Summary of Overcoming Challenges

The team, in its first year of existence, was totally capable of overseeing a new, exciting, growing church. But the major thing that needed work and immediate correction was follow-up and detail planning.

At the beginning of the church launch, each team member was given their specific area of ministry, being admonished to take general oversight seriously, especially their own area. It was recommended to perhaps spend less time on Friday together as a team and use that time for outreach and training.

Good News Africa Gospel Church was accountable to Good Shepherd Africa Gospel Church. The new church let the parent church know what was going on in the new church. The senior pastor of Good Shepherd Church, in his interaction with the team, said reporting back to the mother church would help get the people in the mother church to support the team in every way and also get support and appreciation in what the team was doing. The team, from then on, agreed that it would start giving monthly reports to both the mother church and the denominational headquarters. This was faithfully accomplished from that time.

REFLECTION

It was the new church plant's dream to purchase land by the fifth year of its existence, and within two years to build a multi-purpose hall, which would serve as a place of worship as well as a place for many other activities. Unfortunately, these things did not happen.

The last of the missionary pastors was leaving the daughter church—me. Since I was the senior-most minister of the denomination in Nairobi and the only national, the denominational headquarters pulled me from Good News back to Good Shepherd Church. My family and I returned to the mother church kicking and screaming.

This necessitated the sending of a new pastor to the daughter church. All I can write here is that the choice of the new pastor did not go well with those in Mugoya. For the next ten years, the church struggled. Yet today the church has its own church building and is doing well.

Something we came to know in a new way through this experience was that Jesus is the founder and absolute head of the church. He has been given all power and authority in heaven and on earth. In turn, he has given his church the mandate and authority to go and make disciples of all nations (Matt. 28:19). Jesus reminded us when he said, "The harvest is plentiful, but the laborers are few" (Matt. 9:37-38). Jesus led by example. During his personal ministry here on earth, his focus was always on "the lost sheep," to bring them into his kingdom (Matt. 10:5-6). He made it his business to "seek the lost."

At certain points in the story, we knew that it was easy to sit in our comfortable church. It was difficult to get up and go "make disciples." The church-planting team understood that going into the world and seeking the lost was going to be uncomfortable and so prepared themselves for what they were to face confronting, convincing, convicting of sin, and converting souls.

The team came to understand that a disciple of Jesus Christ is someone who has resolved that, no matter what, Jesus' commands are to be obeyed. The team came to understand that discipleship is not for the weak-hearted. A disciple is one who has counted the costs and is ready to pay the price—and knows that it's worth it in the end.

RAISING CHURCHES FROM RUBBLE

The Well Church, New Zealand

Clint Ussher

The Well Church (or "The Well" for short) is a strategic church plant of the Wesleyan Methodist Church of New Zealand (WMCNZ). After a decade of faithful people praying, The Well was the answer to their prayers as the first WMCNZ church on South Island. Central to the calling and vision of the church is to equip, send, and resource further church plants throughout the South Island and beyond. The Well launched weekly worship gatherings in February 2013. Since that time, The Well has maintained a steady life of worship and witness in Christchurch as a church of 80-100 in weekly worship attendance. I offer the journey of planting The Well as a case study with some initial reflections, insights, and learnings. I focus on the leadership lessons I learned as the church planter and the lessons we learned as a launch team. I move forward by describing some of the challenges and obstacles encountered by the leadership team in planting The Well and how we responded to them. While The Well started out as a "parachute drop" church plant—the majority of team members moving from other countries to help launch the church—we grew from being just a few families in 2012 to a full-blown church which eventually relocated to permanent facilities in 2017.

BACKGROUND AND CONTEXT

Now let me give you a little background on the WMCNZ, which emerged from the Methodist Church of New Zealand in the early 2000s after evangelical reform efforts were thwarted in that denomination. The WMCNZ was established with a renewed commitment to remain part of the Wesleyan/Holiness theological stream with a passion for missional discipleship in the spirit of John Wesley. This was challenging for New Zealand in light of their highly secular and spiritually apathetic culture, with one report ranking New Zealand as the most secular English-speaking nation in the world.[1] From what I can tell, secular influence on the church is evident in declining church involvement across most (if not all) denominational groupings (i.e. Mainline, Evangelical, Independent, and Pentecostal). Yet, in spite of these challenges, the WMCNZ has a strong tradition of planting churches, which continues in the present and exists as a movement of twenty-seven multicultural churches today.

Planting a WMCNZ church in Christchurch was strategic for a number of reasons. Christchurch is the largest city (population of approximately 380,000) and serves as a "gateway" to the South Island, which is home to more than a million people. A vibrant, life-giving Wesleyan church in Christchurch would be well positioned to resource and support further church-planting efforts around the South Island. An evangelical remnant of folks from the Methodist Church affiliated with the WMCNZ from the very beginning and helped keep alive the vision of a WMCNZ church in Christchurch. The legacy of these individuals is one of faithfulness in prayer for many years and continued advocacy for this renewed vision through various obstacles and setbacks. Hence, The Well marks both an answer to prayer and a renewal or rebirth movement in the Wesleyan stream of the church in Christchurch.

STRATEGY AND PROCESS

In November 2009, Rev. Mark Gorveatte (District Superintendent of the West Michigan District of The Wesleyan Church, USA) visited New Zealand to be part of the WMCNZ National Conference as part of an ongoing partnership between WMCNZ and the West Michigan District of The Wesleyan Church. Part of the trip involved a visit with WMCNZ leaders to Christchurch where the vision for "a church that plants churches" was shared and Rev. Gorveatte was consulted on vision, strategy, and possible planters. In that conversation, Rev. Gorveatte offered the names of Clint and Jamie Ussher for consideration. With the endorsement of WMCNZ leaders, Rev. Gorveatte called Clint Ussher on December 9th, 2009 to share the vision and ask if they would prayerfully consider planting a church in Christchurch, beginning a yearlong discernment process.

Catching the Vision

The Usshers were living in Princeton, New Jersey, at the time, where Clint was pursuing M.Div. studies at Princeton Theological Seminary. Clint was also serving (part-time) on staff at Princeton Alliance Church as a licensed minister of the Christian and Ministry Alliance. The phone call with Rev. Gorveatte sparked enough interest for the Usshers to seriously pray and consider the invitation and led to a lengthy discernment journey for both the Usshers and WMCNZ during 2010. This included two visits to New Zealand—first for Clint in June 2010, and subsequently as a whole family (Clint, Jamie, and their two young daughters: Evee and Iris) in October 2010—before the Usshers signed on to lead the new plant.

In February 2011, Christchurch, the "quaint English settlement," suffered unexpected major earthquakes and significant loss of life that devastated the area for years, causing severe trauma and long-term damage to the people and their city. The ground acceleration experienced in February 2011 would totally flatten most world cities, causing massive loss of life. In Christchurch, New Zealand's stringent building codes limited the disaster. Equally (if not more) destructive were the human effects of an event like this. All aspects of life had been disrupted—home, work, social, school, etc.—forcing significant fracturing of communities and relocation. People experienced extremely high levels of stress and economic hardship as they adapted to navigating life in a city filled with ruins. Physical, emotional, and spiritual reserves were spent, and people faced the overwhelming task of rebuilding their lives and city over many years.

It was during the immediate aftermath of the February 2011 earthquakes that the Usshers were engaged in church-planting training in the USA, and the initial vision and plans for The Well began to take shape. As a result of this training, extended prayer, and collective discernment of the vision and mission, a name for the new church emerged from the story of Jesus and the Samaritan woman at the well in John 4. Summarizing their vision in a sentence, The Well seeks to be a church that "awakens people to experience and express the depth of God's love." The remainder of 2011 was spent developing a team of supporters—prayer partners, financial partners, and launch team members from around the world.

The Pre-Launch Phase

In January 2012, the Ussher family relocated from Princeton to Christchurch and began laying the foundations for launching The Well. Before long a small group started gathering weekly on Sundays for a time of worship, prayer, Bible study, and fellowship. As 2012 moved forward, this group studied the life and ministry of Jesus in the Gospel of Luke followed by the life and ministry of the early church in Acts. This, coupled with weekly meals they shared together, served as a wonderful foundation for building community with a missional focus. In July 2012, two families moved from Brisbane, Australia, to join the launch efforts. Their launch team included Logan and Emilie Hoffman from Indiana in the United States. Logan joined Clint in a staff capacity as Assistant Pastor. This group of early adopters, along with the Yeo family (recently moved from Singapore) and the Simpsons, who had prayed for a Wesleyan church to be planted, formed a launch team for The Well.

The early buzz for the launch of The Well grew significantly during the final months of 2012 as the launch date drew closer. After months of prayer-walking different areas of the city, there was a clear leading toward Sydenham, a city-fringe suburb to the south of Christchurch's Central Business District, as the place to establish The Well. Interestingly, the historic stone building of the Sydenham Wesleyan/Methodist Church was reduced to a pile of rubble as a result of the earthquakes (although it had not served as a church for several years prior). The Well offered four "preview services" once each month from October 2012 until January 2013. These provided practice runs for the launch team in preparing and running a Sunday worship service and children's ministry. These were, however, ineffective in reaching many new people. This suggests, perhaps, that traditional sequences for starting a church may not work in a highly secularized society.

The Official Launch

The Well launched weekly worship gatherings on Sunday, February 10th, 2013 in Beckenham School (which was the closest available venue to Sydenham at the time). The early buzz and excitement continued as the church experienced early signs of growth. Team members were actively promoting The Well and inviting friends to come along. The team worked hard to make the Sunday worship gatherings a wonderful experience for guests—with genuine worship, biblical preaching, and an excellent children's ministry program. The Well hosted a weekend retreat in June 2013 that strengthened relationships and sense of community with those who were becoming regulars. This Winter Retreat was such a highlight that it has become an annual event for the community. Further, an early partnership began to form with Beckenham School as an avenue for community outreach. The church and school worked together to host community Christmas celebrations, free family movies during the colder winter months, and Easter egg hunts. The Well also sponsored morning teas with a barista coffee van for school staff and provided lunches for children who came to school without a lunch. On the other hand, an effort to develop a mentoring program with the school failed to come to fruition. In other words, not all efforts in outreach gained traction.

Other key resources in these early stages of The Well included ongoing coaching, encouragement, New Zealand cultural insights, and advice provided by WMCNZ. Being part of a wider network of churches proved very beneficial and provided access to good thinkers and experienced church planters who were instrumental in shaping the early days of The Well. Another key resource was the prayer and financial support of local and international partners. A handful of churches and a large number of individuals committed to financially support The Well for the first three years. The Well Church raised funds to the tune of $300,000 for year one; $250,000 for year two; and $200,000 for year three. In large part, this was due to the incredibly generous support of Princeton Alliance Church, an anchor donor in this project. Their contributions of $100,000 per year for three years and help sponsoring two short-term mission teams enabled The Well to establish itself far more quickly than would have otherwise been possible.

The Well has become known for its worship gatherings and community outreach. On any given Sunday 80-100 people gather in worship. Feedback received from guests and new members at The Well indicates that our Sunday worship is a top strength of the church. In particular, people comment on the church community, saying they are warm, friendly, and welcoming. People also appreciate the depth and relevance of biblical preaching, the genuine spirit of worship, and the quality of the children's ministry offered for children 0-12 years of age.

CHALLENGES

Overcoming "Parachute Drop" Challenges

As with any new endeavor, unique challenges arose. First, the launch team for The Well was faced with the challenges associated with being a "parachute drop" church plant. While valuable support, advice, and encouragement were available from the wider WMCNZ network, the team experienced feelings of isolation due to geographic separation from the rest of the WMCNZ (predominantly in the North Island of New Zealand). The team was largely forced to figure things out for themselves with only a few team members able to offer local knowledge and advice. While this challenge has been, and continues to be, experienced by church planters in other cities around the world, part of this challenge for The Well was overcoming an undercurrent of skepticism and resistance from local people. Christchurch local culture can tend toward parochialism and insularity. Thus, outsiders can be viewed with antipathy or suspicion—attitudes which extended at times to relations with other churches. Whereas some churches experience outward persecution, others like The Well experience resistance of a different kind. While there were some local pastors who were very warm, welcoming, and embracing of The Well, there were a number who were less so—some of whom even expressed resistance to the idea of another church. This only served to reinforce the message that the launch team members of The Well were outsiders. In overcoming this obstacle, The Well would need to cultivate a sense of belonging and trustworthiness. Here's what we did:

1. *Adopting the Humble Posture of a Learner.* In responding to the challenge of being viewed as outsiders, launch team members followed the advice of Pastor David Macgregor (Grace Vineyard Church, Christchurch), who emphasized the importance of com-

ing into the city humbly and adopting the posture of learners. Rather than thinking The Well was God's answer for reaching Christchurch, it was important for The Well to recognize God was at work in Christchurch, and they were simply joining what God had already been doing. This proved doubly important due to the high degree of ecumenical unity and collaboration across the churches in Christchurch. In response, Rev. Clint Ussher met with 85 different local pastors during 2012 to learn about life, ministry, and the post-earthquake context in Christchurch. Not only did this produce valuable understanding of the local context, it also served to develop strong collegial and ecumenical relationships that continue to this day. The launch team was quick to get involved in ecumenical activities right from the outset.

2. *Transitioning to Local Leadership.* The Well launch team worked intentionally to transition from a group of outsiders and newcomers to a team of aligned, mostly local, leadership. One of the most common questions asked around the leadership table was, "How does this fit with Kiwi culture?" Or, stated differently, "Is this the Kiwi way?" There was a concerted effort to draw local people not only into the life of the church but also—and especially—into leadership roles. This occurred over a couple of years (2014-2015). At the same time, it was important to not overlook the value of being an outsider or a newcomer. Outsiders are not "bad." They often provide fresh perspective and insight on matters where local people may be blinded by their own enculturation. After all, the church has always grown through missionary activity. Yet, mission also involves the work of contextualization and developing indigenous ownership. This was the hope and aim for The Well right from the outset, which helped considerably in overcoming some of the skepticism and resistance associated with being outsiders and instead earned early trust and credibility.

3. *From Staff-led to Elder-led.* The transition from a staff-led church to an elder-led church involved some significant gear shifting for The Well. The early leadership consisted of the families of Lead Pastor Clint Ussher, Assistant Pastor Logan Hoffman, and two other families who voluntarily moved from Australia to help launch The Well.

Each of these families relocated to Christchurch to be part of The Well and tell interesting stories in shaping the journey toward local leadership. In different ways, they relate to the parachute drop reality of building a team from scratch with initial support that transitioned away. The story of the Hoffmans is one of valuable short-term development helpers with the overlay of significant personal tragedy (mentioned below). One of the families from Australia tells the story of non-alignment and relational conflict. The other family from Australia really captures the volunteers who became migrants rather than missionaries and themselves moved within New Zealand, relocating to Auckland for work.

Working Through Outsider Challenges

Consisting largely of outsiders or newcomers to Christchurch, the team experienced the cross-cultural clash between their own default assumptions, expectations, and preferences and the cultural norms. The clash was felt across a number of different issues: leadership, the place of the church in society, relationships, and worship styles. The confluence of the gap between the expectations and dreams of the launch team and reality, and the way that played into personality flaws and insecurities, became a major challenge in the early years of The Well. The team had prayed, dreamed, believed, and expected the church to grow steadily and relatively quickly. When that did not occur, it became difficult for the leaders to experience this as anything other than a referendum on their personal leadership and ability. These heightened insecurities exacerbated relational discord among launch team members. As they say in sports, "Winning cures all ills." It is likely the launch team for The Well would have had far fewer clashes over leadership and direction if success had been immediate and visible. Here's what we did to work through these issues:

1. *Taking a More Contextual Approach.* As we responded to the clash between expectations and reality, most of the adjustment required the growth and integration of a more contextual leadership style, particularly on the part of Lead Pastor, Clint Ussher. Having experienced most of his ministry and leadership formation in the US,

Clint's default leadership style was more "out in front," directive, and visionary, and this has required some adjusting to a more collaborative and consensus-building style than would have been natural for him. This has caused frustration as to speed and efficiency. Yet, this "leading from among" style is deeply ingrained in Kiwi culture (highly egalitarian), so it was necessary to adopt it, especially until Clint and the leaders earned some credibility and were no longer viewed as outsiders.

2. *Adjusting Metrics.* It was also important for The Well to adjust their metrics for success. Planting a church in New Zealand is a long and slow process—far longer and slower than anticipated. It became apparent early on that the initial goals and targets for The Well were unrealistic and required revision. The input and advice of WMCNZ National Leaders, Rev. Dr. Richard Waugh, and Rev. Brett Jones was helpful in redefining success based in the highly secular New Zealand context. WMCNZ Leadership proved very encouraging and supportive as The Well navigated these early stages. Their assessment of The Well's progress was generally more positive and encouraging than that of the launch team, especially of the pastors. Such disparate views further reinforced The Well's unrealistic measures for success, which were primarily influenced by the American context in which rapid church growth is more common.

Facing Team Unity Issues and Personal Challenges

As alluded to above, the early years of The Well were plagued by relational conflict and division. Fortunately, the conflict was contained within the leadership team and did not have overt spillover effects on the wider congregation. That does not mean there weren't covert effects experienced by a wider group of people. The conflict began over differences in ministry philosophy and preferences. As time progressed and things remained unresolved, the conflict escalated beyond disagreement on ministry philosophy to personal attacks on character, calling, and capability. The fallout of this conflict was significant on a number of levels. One key family left and moved back to Australia. Lead Pastor Clint Ussher suffered mild-to-moderate depression and heightened insecurity causing second-guessing, uncertainty, and lack of clarity of direction in his leadership. As the famous saying of Bill Hybels goes, "Everything rises and falls on leadership." The Well entered a season of plateau lasting approximately 18 months from late 2014 until early 2016. The initial buzz was long past, and it took all the energy and devotion of the team to simply get through another week.

Beyond relational conflict, there were other significant personal challenges for The Well members to navigate. Logan Hoffman, the Assistant Pastor, had relocated with his wife Emilie from the US to be part of the launch team. Only six months after launching The Well, Logan's dad died in a tragic accident. Logan and Emilie continued to serve faithfully for another 18 months amidst their own grief journey before returning home to be closer to family and to pursue further study and ministerial preparation. In addition to this, Clint Ussher's family was navigating health issues. Clint's father was undergoing chemotherapy cancer treatment in Australia. Continued ministry amidst these circumstances carried a high emotional toll. Here's what happened in response:

1. ***Acknowledging Fallings-Short.*** Efforts to navigate the relational conflict among the launch team were largely unsuccessful. Both pastoral families (the Usshers and the Hoffmans) and both families from Australia were caught up in the conflict that went on for more than 12 months; in the end, however, the conflict really was between Clint and one of the families from Australia. After months of lengthy conversations failed to resolve, both parties felt at an impasse without seeing a way forward. The solution was the return of one family to Australia. As with most conflict, no party was entirely innocent in the exchanges. Things were said that caused significant hurt and offense on both sides of the fence. Trust was delicate and both parties left aiming to keep some level of friendship intact.

2. *Learning from the Past.* In hindsight, this part of The Well's story suggests three lessons:

- A new launch team can be more vulnerable due to lack of trust and shared experiences;
- Forming a team of contemporaries and friends can be a wonderful blessing but requires very candid and open dialogue; and
- Engaging a godly and trusted mediator might have been one way to reach resolution and perhaps regain some of the lost trust.

The hurt and pain experienced necessitated a period of healing and recalibrating. Both Clint and Logan spent time in counseling: Logan to help navigate his grief journey, and Clint to navigate his journey through conflict, depression, and heightened insecurities. Logan also took a period of personal leave away from ministry responsibilities. Clint, who was also pursuing D.Min. studies at the time, deferred his studies for 12 months during 2015 to relieve some of the additional pressure and stress. These were all efforts to see some health restored in the lives of these young leaders. Such journeys toward health are often quite long, and while both leaders would say they are still on the journey, both Clint and Logan are experiencing better health today.

Challenges from Natural Disasters

Finally, while each of the obstacles identified above is significant, perhaps the greatest challenge in planting The Well was the aftermath of the Christchurch earthquakes, which is arguably New Zealand's worst natural disaster. A parachute-drop church plant with a majority of people from other cultures in a city as insular as Christchurch would have been difficult in any case, but doing so in the immediate aftermath of such upheaval with relational conflict, grief, and family health issues was a lot to overcome, to say the least. While the earthquakes presented opportunities for churches in the immediate aftermath, it was actually a challenge in the long term. People were emotionally, spiritually, and physically exhausted, leaving little energy for exploring spiritually. In the aftermath of a tragedy, people tend to go into survival mode, which often means leaving aside anything non-essential. In some parts of the world, it seems that tragedy leads people to seek spiritual answers, but that is not as true in New Zealand. Instead, Kiwis retreat to the things that help life to make sense and help them get through the day, and in New Zealand it seems as if that's a day at the beach or on the boat more than it is a day in church. Whereas the launch team thought that the earthquakes would provide opportunities to have spiritual conversations, the earthquakes actually might have made it more difficult to plant rather than easier. These "disasters" gave us unique opportunities for redemption. Here's what we were able to do:

1. ***Helping with Suicide Prevention.*** While the tragedy of the earthquakes did not produce an immediate spiritual desire in people, it did provide a number of unique opportunities for The Well to respond. One of the first responses developed by The Well was in response to the growing need around suicide prevention and support for those bereaved by suicide. New Zealand has a very high rate of suicide, and Christchurch is no exception. This was true prior to the earthquakes, but the numbers only increased after the earthquakes.

   Jamie Ussher met Theresa in April 2012, soon after the Usshers arrived in Christchurch. Theresa had lost her partner to suicide only three months prior in January 2012. As Jamie started searching with Theresa to find some help and support in her grief, they discovered that support groups for those bereaved by suicide were no longer operating in Christchurch since its funding had been cut in 2007. After further research and much prayer, The Well sponsored Jamie to receive specialist training by Skylight[2] in Wellington to facilitate support groups for people bereaved by suicide. Jamie became a catalyst for getting these started again in Christchurch, and a number of other social and community agencies have also had people trained and joined Jamie in this effort. Since 2012, there have been 2-4 groups running in Christchurch every year serving this very specific need. This unique ministry has opened a number of opportunities for gospel witness and offers for prayer/ministry, and has even seen a handful of folks from these groups join The Well for Sunday worship. Theresa has been through the Alpha Course at The Well and is a regular part of The Well community, still moving forward on her spiritual journey.

2. ***Helping Bolster Foster Care Efforts.*** One other way families from The Well have met needs in the post-earthquake community has been foster care. The need for foster care in Christchurch rose significantly as a result of the earthquakes. There were more children in need of care, usually due to the increased stress and pressure placed on their parents and caregivers in the aftermath of the disaster. Additionally, the number of caregivers in foster care declined as people moved away or no longer had the capacity (due to their own stress, etc.) to provide adequate care for the children entrusted to them. When considering Jesus' call to care for the widows and orphans in the community, The Well recognized children in the foster system to be the Christchurch equivalent of orphans and the need to do something about it. In response, Clint and Jamie Ussher, along with three other families from The Well, became foster caregivers. So throughout the life of The Well, it has been commonly understood that they are a church who cares for "the least of these" (Matt. 25:40), and children in care are regularly part of The Well church community. It has been wonderful for these foster families to encourage and support one another along the fostering journey within the same faith community.

3. ***Purchasing Property.*** The earthquakes also opened the possibility for The Well to purchase their own property. In August 2015, The Well purchased the earthquake-damaged property of the Sydenham Rugby League Football Club. The property is in a prime location and was purchased at land value because the existing building was badly damaged and required a lot of work to repair to become safe for use. This provided a wonderful opportunity to convert the existing building into church facilities. The purchase and building project were made possible through the incredible generosity of a kingdom donor who was eager to see WMCNZ thrive in Christchurch. This donor gifted $300,000 to The Well in order to purchase the property and

then arranged a further $650,000 interest-free loan to finance the building works. The Well would not have been in a position to purchase the property had it not been for the generosity of this kingdom donor. Such generosity and sizeable gifts have not been experienced by other WMCNZ churches and suggests that new church plants often appeal to new donors and supporters. It is important to note the funding was not offered in advance of the building purchase but came only in response to The Well's stepping out in faith.

Part of why the property journey is so significant for The Well is a further response to the post-earthquake context in Christchurch. After the earthquakes, people experienced so much disruption and transience in their lives—schools, workplaces, cafes, clubs, and homes all experienced damage and were either closed or relocated—and all aspects of life were affected. This grew a greater appreciation for places and spaces for the people of Christchurch. The Well hopes that having their own permanent facilities will strengthen their sense of permanence and belonging in the community, and perhaps help further overcome the stigma of being outsiders. Furthermore, it will provide opportunity for The Well to support, encourage, and resource other church plant projects.

To date, The Well has been involved in supporting two church plants—Journey Church in Dunedin, and Church 360 in Swannanoa (North Canterbury). Pastor Clint also consults and coaches with a number of potential church plants further afield in Auckland, Wellington, Hamilton, and Southland. It has always been the hope for The Well to support and catalyze church-planting efforts of the WMCNZ around the South Island, so it is encouraging to see early growth in this direction.

REFLECTION

When reflecting on the process of planting The Well, it seems there were a number of reasons the church survived and beat the odds we have heard about for parachute-drop church plants! Let me list a few here:

- The legacy of prayer that preceded The Well. People prayed for a decade before and continued in regular rhythms of prayer together after The Well was launched.
- The significant financial investment of overseas supporters. You can weather a lot of storms when you're able to keep paying the bills. Without such a strong support base, The Well would not be in the position they are today.
- The launch team adopted the posture of learners. They made intentional efforts to assimilate local people who were early adopters into established team members.
- The regular encouragement and support of WMCNZ National Leaders for the church planter and launch team was vital. This points to the importance of healthy support networks for church planters in caring for themselves but also the wider plant team.
- The grit, determination, and perseverance of The Well leadership were key. This kept them going when the odds were stacked against them, even when their efforts seemed futile. This suggests that resilience is a high characteristic for church planters and church-planting teams.

There were a number of things that did not go well in this church plant. The initial preview services proved ineffective and may have begun too early in the process. Similarly, weekly worship gatherings may have launched too soon and without the necessary critical mass for sustainability. It likely would have been better to build a larger core group or groups pre-launch in order to start with a larger number of people. If we had done these things, The Well may have broken through some of the early growth barriers sooner in their journey. Rather than taking four and half years to get to the point they are now at the time of writing, they may have reached 60-70 people in core groups in 18-24 months which would have enabled a much stronger launch and greater likelihood of growing past 100 in weekly worship within the first six months post-launch.

Looking Forward with Lessons from the Past

In order to become more fruitful, The Well has recently revamped their Life Groups. They are also joining a 3DM Learning Community to clarify their discipleship pathway.[3] The approach to growing missional disciples at The Well has, to date, been somewhat haphazard and ad hoc. That is not to say nothing has been happening. There is evidence of people growing and maturing in Christ. It is, instead, a reflection that disciple making has been more accidental than intentional for us. Early fruit resulting from this change is evident in improved discipleship conversations (improved in both quality and quantity) in Life Groups and deeper integration of faith into people's lives. There is also an increased openness to invited accountability around matters of spiritual growth. Leaders of The Well have a growing sense that well-discipled Christ followers are the greatest opportunity for ongoing gospel witness and evangelistic efforts. This challenge is not unique to The Well; the wider church in New Zealand (NZ) is facing this as well, asking, "What does fruitful and faithful gospel witness look like in our context?" This question remains unresolved at The Well, in the sense that while not declining like the majority of NZ churches, they have very few instances of people coming directly to a saving knowledge of Jesus Christ and giving their lives to follow him. In order to see this trend change, The Well leaders are working hard to clarify an intentional discipleship pathway of multiplying missional disciples.

Part of the uniqueness of the story of The Well is how it was the result of a global church-planting partnership that crossed borders and denominational lines. The partnership between WMCNZ and the West Michigan District of The Wesleyan Church (USA) served to provide valuable resourcing for identifying, assessing, and training church planters that extends to a number of other WMCNZ churches. It is a story of profound collaboration and sacrifice. It has also led to the connection between WMCNZ and the Usshers. Furthermore, the Usshers' journey through the Christian and Missionary Alliance over ten years in the US led to partnership with others who shared a similar heart and passion for church planting, including an anchor financial supporter in Princeton Alliance Church who made significant investments in launching The Well. Existing relational links to individuals and churches in Australia, particularly the Wesleyan Methodist Church of Australia, resulted in prayer and financial support for The Well. In one sense, these are unique factors, but in another sense, they may suggest considerable power in the possibility of synergies like this for future church-planting initiatives around the world.

RECLAIMING THE MISSING GENERATION

G2, North of England

Christian Selvaratnam

The church G2[1] began as an experiment to see if a church meeting in a neutral location, outside of the typically ancient and austere buildings of the Church of England, might connect with a new group of people who avoid church. Thousands of experimental new mission initiatives like G2 have been established to reach people outside of the culture of existing and typically traditional forms of church. These initiatives are termed "fresh expressions of church," a phrase which refers to a broad range of pioneering mission initiatives. "Fresh expressions" are focused on people outside of existing churches and aim to become mature expressions of church shaped by the gospel and the enduring marks of the church. Launching from the Church of England in 2004, the Fresh Expressions movement now encompasses five denominations and fourteen partner organizations in the UK and more than eight countries around the world.[2]

The city of York has an ancient history in Christianity. The Venerable Bede writes about Christian converts in York in the early second century and Roman Christianity in York dates back to the late second century. The Roman Emperor, Constantine the Great, allegedly converted to Christianity in 312 A.D. in York. The seventh century "Northern Saints"—St. Paulinus, St. Aidan, St. Hilda and St. Cuthbert—have all left their mark on the city of York and surrounding region as traveling evangelists and missionaries, with many ancient church buildings bearing their names. The city remains the capital of the northern ecclesiastical province of the Church of England.

St. Michael le Belfrey, a parish church in the city of York situated next to the cathedral, planted G2.[3] A church called St. Michael le Belfrey existed as early as the eighth century[4], and the present building originally served wealthy merchants and local craft-guilds. Rebuilt in the 1500s, it is currently the largest parish church in the city.

By the 1960s, the congregation of St. Michael le Belfrey had diminished to just over ten people and plans to turn the church into a museum were considered. In 1965, David Watson became the vicar of St. Cuthbert's Church in York, which had fewer than a dozen people in attendance at any service. His gifted leadership and preaching revived the congregation to the point where, eight years later, they had outgrown the St. Cuthbert's building. The Archbishop invited him to move this congregation half a mile to St. Michael le Belfrey, in order to replant that church. The congregation continued to grow and many hundreds attended services within a few years of the move. Watson assumed a national and international role in evangelism, student missions and ecumenism. In the 1980s, his friendship with John Wimber[5] helped catalyze a movement of charismatic renewal in the Church of England with far-reaching effects.

Other fresh expressions started by St. Michael le Belfrey include a Chinese church reaching Mandarin speaking university students and restaurant workers; "visions," offering alt:worship[6] for clubbers; "transcendence," a service exploring ancient liturgy with contemporary production; "conversations," a church for graduates meeting in a vodka bar; and two re-plants into nearby declining parishes.

The modern city of York has a population of 200,000 people, including many UK and international students across two universities. The historic industries of the railways and confectionery trade gave way to tourism and service industries. Roman walls ring the city and encompass many medieval churches, including the cathedral church of the Diocese and Province. At least thirty new churches have started in York in the last thirty years, many outside of the traditional denominations, although the overall church-going population still declined in that period.[7]

ABOUT G2

G2 launched in 2004, following a year of preparation: surveys of unchurched friends, prayer walking, profiling patrons at a local health-club gym, which became the first meeting place of the church plant. For the first few years, G2 held café-style services and organized the meeting space around banquet tables, which acted as the gathering point for hospitality and discussion. Congregation members dipped in and out of the meeting as they wished for refreshments—and, during the first month, newspapers—made available throughout the meeting.

From the outset, G2 offered something different: an experience to contrast the local Anglican churches and an approach that connected with those unconnected with a church. In the spirit of being fresh, we experimented with different forms of communication, preaching style, patterns of worship, and room layout. A meeting about Holy Communion included twelve automatic bread-makers hidden in the room and timed to produce fresh bread in time for a Eucharist experience around tables. A service called "Naked Bible" consisted of a New Testament book reading, performed as a dramatic piece. Four people delivered their first short sermons on "Ignition Sunday." In a meeting called "Zones," members of the congregation chose which combination of elements they attended, having been offered a menu of talks, worship experiences, and prayer activities.

G2 experimented in church management and leadership as well as public meetings. Particularly in working with a younger generation, willingness to try different ways of ordering the governance and ministry-development of church life has had a significant effect. This has included a high permission-giving approach to congregation members interested in starting new ministry projects and a deliberate focus on involving as many people as possible in different areas of church life. Individual church members established virtually all of the mission and social action projects of the church at the grassroots level, and a culture of missional entrepreneurship extends throughout the church.

Today, G2 is a mature and thriving church of over 250 adults and children. It has recently planted out another church and has plans for further planting in the coming years. Six people from G2 have been accepted for ordination in the Church of England[8] and G2 has sent out a number of young leaders who are now actively involved in other churches and church plants around the country. Some current members of G2 hold positions of significant seniority in local and national Christian organizations, and G2 has an unusually high level of influence in church culture, disproportionate to its size.[9]

A distinctive feature of G2 is its age profile. More than 80 percent of the adults involved are under the age of thirty. The proximity of two local universities has provided an ongoing stream of young adults who have joined the church. Many have remained part of the church after university, and some have now become young families within the congregation. It is worth noting that, compared with the wider Church of England, G2 is an unusually youthful church. For example, the "Everyone Counts" survey of Church of England parishes and congregations, carried out in 2014, identified that, "A person aged between seventy-six and eighty-five is 8 times more likely to attend a Church of England church than a person aged between eighteen and twenty-four."[10] This significant generational decline in the established church has resulted in some referring to millennials as the "Missing Generation."[11]

In G2, a large proportion of these millennial-aged church members are involved in leadership and ministry, either in Sunday services, mid-week groups, work-place activities, evangelistic projects, or social action and social justice initiatives. These emerging leaders are typically young: the modal age of preachers and worship leaders in a typical Sunday meeting is 22, and the mean age of the recent church plant team was 24. Men and women are equally represented in public ministry roles, and virtually all of these young leaders have held their first leadership or ministry role at G2. Moreover, very few have transferred from other local churches.[12]

The leadership development model of G2 has been based on the idea of apprenticeship. Prospective new leaders are given the opportunity to work alongside an existing leader as mentees, or they have the opportunity to try ministry under supervision—for example, giving a short talk. Many new leaders have developed into effective leaders and ministers through a simple experience-reflection framework, with coaching and support provided before the task followed by feedback and reflection afterwards.

For the purpose of this paper, the term "millennial"[13] refers to young adults who turned 18 years old on or after the millennial year—2000 A.D.—equating to people, at the time of writing this, who are in their late teens through to mid-thirties. The G2 experience is of predominantly white British-born university-educated millennials. It is noted, though outside the scope of this paper, that the term "millennials" is likely to have different application in the UK than in the US, and that some would want to argue for a division of the term in to further sub-categories. It is used here as a broad label for a specific age group that is significantly under-represented in church attendance.

CHALLENGES

Opposition from Those Who Expect an Attractional Church Culture

In the early years, the leaders of G2 noticed a cultural challenge when new people were given the opportunity to try preaching, leading a service or worship-leading. It became evident that some older[14] church members found it hard to accept new people leading meetings and preaching, especially when those people were either young or still learning. Some older church members regarded these new leaders as a poor substitute for an ordained minister, an older leader, or a younger leader who had already proved themselves. For example, some older church members took sermon notes for the specific purpose of giving critical feedback to new preachers.

These older church members were following an "attractional church" model—the norm of many British churches—which is a "come to church because it's good" model.[15] "Attractional church"[16] refers to a model often observed in the West, where evangelism functions to draw people into existing church meetings. Typically, the result is that an attractional church becomes focused on the quality of its public meetings. There is, of course, nothing wrong with this model; it is the underlying mode of most churches, especially in historic denominations. However, the attractional model does create a challenge when raising new leaders in the local church, as it requires leaders to be skilled before they can be employed. Because of this, attractional churches must have effective in-house leadership training programs, rely on using leaders who have been trained in other churches, or rely on ordained leaders who have been trained at theological college. An unintended consequence of the attraction model, particularly in a church plant, is that it demands that ministry leaders are already qualified to lead.

An early milestone for G2 was challenging the meme of attractional culture. Their apprenticeship model for developing new leaders provided an effective and simple leadership-development pipeline, but it also conflicted with some cultural assumptions of how public ministry should operate. This raises the following questions: Should the ordained minister be the main preacher and service leader? Should emerging leaders be formally trained before being used? Do people go to church because the ministry is high quality?

The Absence of a Mentoring Culture in Clergy

The ordained minister of G2, and many established church leaders—typically older than the millennial generation—often did not experience personal mentoring in their own formative years.[17] Older clergy typically began their ministerial formation at theological college and had little ministry exposure in the local church prior to selection for ordination training.[18] Whilst some have had the encouragement of being identified and nurtured by an older leader when they were an emerging leader in the local church, most have not. Most older clergy have not experienced a mentoring culture in the local church, which makes it challenging for them to provide this experience for others. This experience of having a spiritual mentor is instinctively sought out by many millennials at G2. Perhaps the influence of mentoring in business, personal trainers for fitness, and coaches for life-style have made the concept of a spiritual director or disciple-making pastor seem normal and necessary.

There is a cost to raising leaders in the local church, particularly in a small plant with limited capacity for training courses. During the early years of a new plant, the training experience inevitably takes place on-the-job, and this presents a risk to the church plant leader. That leader will face a dilemma: Are they the trusted public minister for that church? Is the church plant leader expected to lead service, preach, and lead worship, or are they raising up other leaders to share these tasks? An additional challenge that church planters might face is that many emerging millennial-aged leaders, by virtue of their youth, will be stepping out for the first time with limited prior training. G2 has had its own examples of leaders who are learning through their mistakes in the public sphere: a poor first sermon for a new speaker; a meeting leader who accidentally swore in his opening prayer; and a service unfortunately modeled on the Arian heresy which needed to be properly addressed. Any planter raising a new team of leaders manages the risks that arise when developing keen millennials into effective leaders.

When the answer to the question "who raised you up?" is no one, ordained ministers and senior leaders may be instinctively associating the formative process of leadership with the institutional elements of theological training, rather than the opportunities afforded by the church plant. Overcoming this perception is hard. Ministers who were not mentored themselves will inevitably find it hard to mentor others. Pride and ego war against an established minister who is offering an advantage or opportunity to a young leader that they were not given themselves. Some ministers can, and do, overcome this challenge. In the best examples, this means that church plant leaders genuinely search for leaders who will eventually outshine them, but insecure ministers can easily end up creating assistants rather than successors, or simply leaving leadership formation to the academy.

Extended Adolescence

Over the last thirteen years, G2 has gained significant insight into the characteristics of millennials who have been part of the church. One key observation regards life maturity. Based on my observations, millennials are extending their adolescence into their early 30s. Compared to their parents at the same age, millennials often delay major life decisions such as marriage, having children, and career choices. It is common to meet millennial graduates at G2 who can't decide where to work, millennial couples who are waiting many years to start a family, or millennials in long-term romantic relationship which do not seem to be leading to marriage. There are, no doubt, many reasons why this might happen, but an observed lack of certainty about doctrine and church role is unsurprising when the general ambiguity of life some millennials experience is taken into consideration.

When identifying candidates for leadership opportunities, this lack of clarity can make these younger potential leaders seem less qualified. The temptation, especially for the older church leader calibrated to their own generational norms, is to wait until they mature before they are invited to lead.

So how and where should we distinguish between parts of millennial culture which are good or neutral and those which are weak and need challenging? For example, the millennial general tendency to tolerate the mixing of doubt and belief could be seen as healthy realism, but it could also be seen as ideological consumerism, where a person accepts beliefs only so far as they are personally convenient.

The Challenge and Opportunity of Spiritual Honesty

For millennials, it seems that the days of feeling pressure to adhere to a certain set of Christian doctrines is gone. Labels such as "evangelical," which point to a package of doctrines and systematic beliefs, no longer have the same meaning. Millennials are more spiritually honest and happier than their parents' generation to express their doubts along with their beliefs. Such honesty was evident particularly in the first twelve years of G2, when meetings were café-style and all sermons included table discussion, in which people could express their thoughts and views. Part of the spiritual questioning experienced by millennials may be linked to lower levels of biblical literacy. Anecdotal observations suggest that millennials know far less about the Bible than their parents did at the same age but are more naturally gifted in communication and presentation skills. For example, G2 finds that new millennial-aged preachers typically have great vision, passion, and communication skills but significantly less Bible knowledge than their parents' generation.[19]

One of the gifts to G2 was the absence of any paid staff for a number of years. As in many churches, it was necessary that everyone played a part in the running of the church: all volunteers were welcome and everyone was needed. This inclusive approach proved to be very appealing to the millennial mindset and inviting participation early had the effect of connecting them to church. It seemed that rather than wanting to attend a "perfect church," millennials wanted to be involved in building and shaping their church. That is, to be invited to contribute toward defining the character of the church in which they were involved. G2 found that millennials become committed to churches built by them, not for them. Despite the fact that millennials are the "Missing Generation" for some churches, G2 has found that millennials are interested in church where they can play a formational role. The painful truth is that while they might not be interested in a particular church, if the church culture fits, they may join.

Millennials seem to engage with church leadership in a different way from their parents' generation. For example, during one of the early years of G2, a minister informally surveyed the congregation in order to answer the question, "Should I wear my dog-collar on Sunday?" Church members in their 40s and 50s were universally keen that he wore it because it clarified who was in charge and helped their visitor friends know G2 was a trustworthy church. Millennials responded very differently. Some didn't know he was ordained and few seemed bothered: a typical answer was "wear it if you want to." To the millennials, the minister's dog-collar—the uniform that confirms their theological training and selection as a spiritual leader—doesn't accord them with an automatic trustworthiness and authority in the same way that it typically does to older generations. Millennials, it seems, don't have "trusted ministers" in church in the same way as their parents did.

RESPONSE

Three broad ideas have helped shape the culture of G2. They summarize key observations about the distinctive way G2 has operated and seen growth and development as a church.

The Teaching Hospital

In a teaching hospital, young practitioners learn under supervision by being immersed in a role for which they are unprepared. Before they enter the treatment room, the students have most likely read up on the procedure, been briefed by a qualified person, had the opportunity to ask questions, and taken comfort in being amidst a team of equally unqualified learners. During the procedure, they are reassured that a senior medic is in the room, perhaps taking the lead or just supervising. Students take notes on everything and afterwards they reflect on their experience and what they learned.

Perhaps church plants need to function more like a teaching hospital, where emerging leaders can learn by "doing ministry" under supervision and with excellent support and feedback. This approach requires a significant shift in expectations for older generations, but attracts millennials. Church members who have been involved in a ministry are far less likely to be critical of their church, often tending to be more committed and more supportive of others who are growing in ministry. Just as a teaching hospital represents a cultural shift from regular hospitals, perhaps a church that wishes to be effective in raising millennial leaders needs to pursue a similar cultural shift.

The simple apprenticeship model of leadership development at G2 has been very effective, particularly in developing younger leaders. Older leaders often prefer to have training courses and theological training first—and these things are very important. However, G2 has found that millennials thrive when they are invited to join the team and given opportunities quickly. One millennial, who is now a regular speaker at very large Christian events, remembers many people telling her as a teenager, "One day she might be a good speaker." An existing leader said the same to her during one of her early visits to G2 but also invited her to give a short talk in a few weeks' time. He was the first person to give her an opportunity to exercise her emerging gift.[20]

This relational model of apprenticeship, or coaching, is especially powerful when made visible to the congregation. For example, when a new speaker delivers their first talk, the person who has helped them with their preparation might also introduce the new preacher before they speak. With careful thought, such an introduction can subtly communicate that this person has received suitable support and their contribution has been checked and authorized by a trusted person.

G2 church life and church services are deliberately organized to create opportunities for people to try ministry. A service in which several new people give a short talk is regularly held; each week, two people lead the service (one experienced leader and one in training); and anyone can volunteer to be a leader within the mid-week group system. In all of these examples, emerging leaders are always being stretched—G2 ministry gives people roles and opportunities beyond their own ability to grow them into leadership.

Millennials at G2 are more open, malleable, and enquiring than their parents' generation. In spiritual formation, it is easier to mold something unset. This model has also proved to be self-perpetuating: leaders who have been apprenticed value the experience and find it natural to provide the same opportunity to others. After a while, a culture of apprenticeship forms. It is not uncommon for a 21-year-old to have a 24-year-old ministry mentor.

LEADING FROM THE MIDDLE

"Leading from the middle"[21] is a phrase used by the minister leading G2 to describe a set of learnings for church leaders and planters working with millennials:

- *To raise up millennials, the minister can't be the hero.* Every church planter needs to decide if they are raising assistants or successors: assistants lift the mentor up, but successors go beyond the mentor. As church planters, we have found that it helps to pursue a people-focused church management wherever possible, creating roles around people and giving volunteers as much say as possible. Rather than asking people to serve (in a pre-defined role), we ask them the question, "What's your dream?"
- *Separating church style from church theology creates an innovative church culture.* Churches can be thought of as either open or closed, meaning a church is typically conservative in doctrine and conservative in practice (closed), or liberal in doctrine and liberal in practice (open). A helpful illustration is the "two handed

approach."[22] A church can be like an open hand (which is liberal), or like a closed hand (which is conservative). Whilst G2 is conservative in theology, it has sought to have a liberal approach to ministry practice that is orthodox in doctrine but open to experimenting in style. This is symbolized by one hand open and one hand closed.[23]

- *A minister working with millennials must be a strong reflective practitioner and should teach and release emerging leaders to do the same.* Working with millennials in a denomination where there is little experience within that age group requires space and time for learning. It is also helpful for emerging leaders to learn how to gather and respond to feedback, how to think innovatively, and how to benefit from the discipline of personal retreats.

- *Emerging leaders can be treated as "secret curates."* Clergy are familiar with the practice of training a newly ordained priest (titled "assistant curates") through broad and varied experiences of ministry, supervision, and mentoring. The same principles can be applied very effectively to key emerging leaders, without making assumptions about title and future role.

SPIRITUAL PARENTING

As explained above, one of the challenges of working with some millennials is that they can often have a lower biblical literacy and can also live in a state of extended adolescence. This can stall the cycle of leadership development if the older leader is waiting until all the required aspects of maturity are in place. Millennials, especially those who are emerging as leaders, need spiritual parenting to help them learn how to grow into maturity. It can be helpful for older congregation members and older church leaders to *think of millennials as being in a third developmental stage* after childhood and youth. This is not condescension but rather a recognition that they are still developing.[24]

Here are a few observations we've made with regard to spiritual parenting:

- *Millennials need relational mentors.* Group learning and classroom training are of great help, but millennials often thrive when given individual support from a more mature leader.
- *Millennials need help to protect them from the negative impact of ministry mistakes.* They need to be encouraged to make mistakes and see successes and failures as having equal value—if reflected on—for the sake of self-leadership development. They also need the active support from their mentors as they learn. If leadership goes well they need positive feedback; if they make a mistake, their mentor should limit their exposure to the consequences of their mistakes.
- *Pastors who believe that women should be leaders need to be proactive in deliberately raising them as leaders.* In the UK, it is common for pastors and clergy to have an egalitarian view of women in church leadership, but for the ministry profile of their church and Sunday meetings to not reflect this belief.
- *Involving a millennial in a ministry role is a very easy way to develop an emerging leader.* If this is done well and the young leaders are ready to learn, the emerging leaders will both develop themselves and reproduce the practice in others.

REFLECTION

G2 has developed over thirteen years to become an innovative and growing Anglican church, with a distinctively young congregation. The church plant began as an experiment to reach a new group of people and this has resulted in a strong connection with millennial-aged adults, many of whom are learning to lead and have an appetite for church planting. G2 carries a youthful hope for the future of the church that is noticeably different from the denominational norm, and some of this has been reflected in a first church plant and future aspirations for planting in the city and the region. G2 has excelled in raising younger leaders and is now well known for the quality and abundance of emerging leaders in the congregation.

One of G2's challenges is that it lacks older people—only 20 percent of adults at G2 are over thirty years of age and only a handful are over fifty. This has at times left G2 looking and feeling like a student church. Practically, this means there is a scarcity of mentors and role models for younger members, but more importantly it reflects an intergenerational poverty in the congregational balance. Deeper engagement with Anglican thought is still needed, particularly in exploring Eucharistic life and the liturgical shape and content of public worship. G2 hasn't yet found its full Anglican identity as something distinctively new but also part of the family of churches in the Diocese and the Church of England. While the "Fresh Expression of Church" framework offers useful encouragement and training on starting a Fresh Expression of Church such as G2, it provides little advice or answers on bringing them to maturity as developed forms of church that remain true to their entrepreneurial heritage. Evangelistically, G2 has done well connecting with de-churched adults but less well with the un-churched. The un-churched, who represent the post-Christendom culture, are an increasing proportion of society that may need a more radical approach to be evangelized in large numbers.

One key next step for G2 is to explore a multi-site[25] model of church, alongside exploring more in church planting. Leadership development has reached a stage that G2 needs to create speaking opportunities for emerging preachers. Whilst any church can grow capacity by moving to a bigger venue, the limited number of large meeting venues in the city and the desire to retain a strong community vibe in services suggests that a multi-site approach may provide a healthy way for G2 to grow. This would also provide a framework for exploring different innovations concurrently and may complete and multiply the founding story of G2: an emerging experiment to see if a church meeting in a different location, with a different style of meeting, might connect with a new group of people who do not currently go to church.

BRINGING THE GOSPEL HOME

King of Kings Ministries, Israel

Wayne Hilsden

"When it's time to start the church in Jerusalem would you and Ann come and help us?" That's the question pastor Jim Cantelon blurted out to me in 1981. Initially, we dismissed it as a crazy idea. We had thought we were *living the dream*: I was a young pastor at the Stone Church, just a few blocks from the University of Toronto and Wycliffe College, where I had recently graduated; the young adults' ministry I was leading was growing, and this group was radically renewing the face of the church; and my wife, Ann, was the music director of Canada's leading Christian television ministry. We were experiencing great effectiveness in ministry.

But we couldn't shake that invitation to help plant a church in Jerusalem—even though we had never been to Israel before. So we decided to go on a "spy out the land" tour in December 1981, the same year Jim posed that challenging question to us. This trip enabled us to pray more intelligently about the invitation. On that ten-day trip we felt a strong sense of God's leading, and in August of 1983 we made our move to Israel, along with our two pre-school sons, Jamie and Joel.

We were barely off the plane when we began to co-lead a home fellowship with Jim Cantelon and his wife (also Canadians). Less than twenty people gathered for this fellowship in those first few weeks, and that number included the nine members of our two Canadian families. Nevertheless, this little home fellowship would form the core group of our first church plant, what is now known as King of Kings Community, Jerusalem (www.kkcj.org).

At that time, most ministries were engaged in work among Israel's Arab population. However, we sensed something different for our ministry: that our primary calling was to minister among the Jewish community of Israel. We saw in Galatians 2:9 a precedent in which the Jerusalem "pillars" were called primarily to the Jews and the apostle Paul mostly to the Gentiles. So with our sense of calling in this direction, we decided to grow King of Kings Community in a predominantly Jewish area of the city, just west of the Old City walls.

Our Greatest Challenge

The most significant challenge we have faced is seventeen centuries of "Christian" anti-Semitism—rooted in a supersessionist interpretation of the Scriptures, which assumes that God replaced the Jews with a new chosen people, the Church—and that the covenants he made with Israel are now invalid. Our commitment to proclaim the gospel created apprehension among many of the people we came to bless. Most Jews have historically viewed the Christian message as an existential threat and reject it outright, perceiving it as possibly the most sinister form of anti-Semitism of all.

Strategy and Process: Starting an "International" Plant

Our first plant, King of Kings Community, was English-speaking, in part because Israeli officials gave us clergy visas on the assumption that we would be an international church that serves pilgrims and expatriates. Indeed, a large percentage of our early expatriate adherents served in parachurch ministries based in Jerusalem. There were also UN and Consulate personnel who gravitated to our new plant. As the congregation grew, it became increasingly known around the world for its vibrant worship and music. Consequently, King of Kings Community was a magnet for visitors. This phenomenon, however, caused some Israelis to feel like strangers on their own soil.

At first, the international character of King of Kings Community seemed a distraction from our primary calling. It took nearly a decade before we came to appreciate how an English-speaking congregation could play a strategic role in connecting the nations to Israel and fulfill a biblical mandate of the church—"to make Israel envious" (Rom. 11:11). We also began to see how our partnerships with churches and individuals around the world were providing significant resources to enable us to expand our reach.

Another significant development under the umbrella of an English-speaking congregation was the inclusion of Hebrew-speaking home groups within the small group network at King of Kings. Some of these home groups eventually became congregations.

Numerical Growth and Leadership Changes

A month and a half after our launch we moved from the apartment to a small rented hall. A year and a half later an opportunity arose to obtain a long-term lease on the 600-seat concert hall of the YMCA on King David Street. The Jerusalem Symphony Orchestra had decided to end their multi-decade contract at the YMCA, so their Sunday evening slot became available. We saw this as providential. The auditorium was across the street from the famed King David Hotel. We signed on the dotted line, and it became our worship center for about 20 years. By the mid-1990s, this hall was nearly filled each Sunday evening.

A significant change happened in 1988 when our fellow Canadian colleagues, Jim and Kathy Cantelon, sensed the Lord leading them back to Canada. I had been the co-pastor from the beginning, but with their departure, I became the senior pastor. Our vision had always been to plant congregations and train leaders, so I went looking for someone with experience in these areas. I discovered Dr. Ray Gannon, a pioneer in the US messianic movement, who had planted several congregations and had teaching experience at a seminary.

When Ray joined us, we were already in discussions with several other ministries to establish a national Bible college. Such a consortium would soon prove impossible. Consequently, we initiated the launch of King of Kings College (now called Israel College of the Bible). Our goal from the beginning was to raise up local indigenous leaders to take charge of the college, and within the first five years, this came to fruition. Since its beginning in 1990, more than two thousand Israelis have attended the College. Several hundred have graduated with bachelor's or master's degrees. In 2017, the College launched a Doctor of Ministry degree program in cooperation with Dallas Theological Seminary.

A Major Shift: Purchasing Our Facilities

In the early 2000s, I went to Galilee on a personal retreat. I was desperate for God's direction—and I had been feeling inadequate to the task. That's when I had a powerful and life-changing experience with the Holy Spirit. I emerged from that supernatural encounter with a new dimension of faith, confident that God was leading us to purchase our own worship center in Jerusalem.

We found an old movie theater that had been abandoned for eleven years. Before signing a purchase contract, I invited seven other pastors and leaders in Jerusalem to look at the property and pray for God's will for this place. This gathering turned into a spontaneous worship session. In the end, all agreed that King of Kings should take the bold step and purchase this property. Many miracles ensued, and eventually 8.5 million dollars came in to buy and renovate the facility.

We named this worship and conference center The Pavilion. Rather than attach our King of Kings branding, we believed that a more generic name would help other ministries share the vision and not feel that they would have to join King of Kings in any official way to benefit from it.

Over the next thirteen years, King of Kings Ministries acquired over thirty title deeds in the same building, including the entire top floor of this seventeen-story building, where we created what we call the Jerusalem Prayer Tower. Today, dozens of ministries enjoy the use of our facilities. At any given time, there are twelve or more congregations that gather in our various auditoriums. Many of these spaces serve as incubators for new church plants.

While our strategic properties have allowed significant kingdom expansion and impact, we regard the more unknown and quiet work of making disciples and developing leaders as central to our work. Even after establishing Israel College of the Bible, our King of Kings leadership team has continued to meet regularly with potential church planters one-on-one.

The Dynamics of Finances and Ministry at KKC

The local people do participate in tithes and offerings in the mother congregation and the smaller ones that have grown from it as well. This does not cover all of the costs. Purchasing the facility that we renovated has been costly. Just the theater itself, the purchase and renovation, was 8.5 million dollars. So it is miraculous. The money came from all over the world. We didn't push hard, but we told our story in many places around the world.

Today, one-third of our income comes through commercial enterprises; we rent out our facilities to various people—not just believing groups, but the wider cultural community. Seven high schools each June are using it for their graduation. We have ballets, concerts, and all kinds of things happening there. So, I'd say it's one-third, one-third, and one-third. One-third is money generated through our congregational engagement, and then one-third comes from the nations.

People have asked how intentional we were about doing commercial enterprises. My answer is that we didn't have any plan to build our own worship center. So for 20 years we were a portable church. We were hauling equipment over to the YMCA every week. It was only after my personal revival that I could believe we could even do that. Once we moved to the building, we just fell into opportunities to purchase significant properties. And then we wanted a front porch to our ministry center, and that was the Café. So, it's really just to say to our neighbors: "We're not a cult. We're not totally weird. Only partially weird!" So Israelis meet us in the cafe context and see that we're running a good business and that we're friendly and there to help.

Church Growth Because of Commercial Enterprises?

Concerning whether we see concrete growth resulting through marketplace ministry: it's limited. We haven't seen as much as we would want. What has happened is that our relationship with the government has changed radically. For example, a former deputy mayor of Jerusalem has now become close friends with my wife, and they have coffee and both have the vision to see this whole building transformed. So that's allowed us to have greater favor and more freedom for all of the other gospel-related ministry we do.

I will say that clergy visas are very hard to get. We personally were fortunate to have clergy visas for the first 18 years. We are now permanent residents as of two years ago—and that was a miracle in itself.

Working Through Adversity

Not every plant succeeded as hoped. The first planting initiative was less than stellar. It began four years after King of Kings got its own start. It began with gifted, but inexperienced planters who were determined to launch with or without the blessing of our King of Kings' leadership. Jim Cantelon and I would often talk to them about the day that they would start their own congregations.

Not unlike many Israeli believers at that time, some of them had an independent spirit. Unwilling to wait until they had a viable plan and the full partnership of King of Kings Community, they went ahead and started. We chose not to hold them back but released them with blessing, with the hope that they would learn on-the-job and that God would give them success, even if the timing appeared to be premature.

Several years later the plant reached a peak of about 70 members. Sadly, due to a divided vision and relational challenges, the new congregation declined. Discouraged, the remaining pastor agreed to a merger with another Hebrew-speaking congregation in Jerusalem. Nevertheless, most of the members of the original plant eventually withdrew from the new hybrid.

The leaders of King of Kings Community learned a valuable lesson from this experience. We determined that we would be more prayerful and would identify and appoint anointed and equipped servant-leaders. Also, we decided that in future endeavors we would maintain a much closer relationship with these pioneers.

We've dealt with other challenges, as well:

- *Cross-Cultural and Linguistic Barriers.* Another challenge we faced was adapting to a foreign language and culture. Ann and I devoted much of our early years to learning Hebrew. We also placed our sons in Hebrew-language public schools and encouraged our ministry colleagues to do the same. It took three years until I could preach, as well as teach, in Hebrew.
- *Ostracism of New Believers.* A significant challenge in making disciples and planting congregations in Israel is the ostracism experienced by Israeli Jews who accept the claims of Jesus. Most new Jewish believers, once they openly share their faith, are spurned even by their loved ones.
- *A Limited Pool of Indigenous Leaders.* Messianic Jewish leaders in Israel in the early 1980s were mostly first-generation believers. A large percentage of them were immigrants from western nations. Consequently, they were not equipped sufficiently to relate cross-culturally even to their fellow Jews in Israel. In our early years, we regularly sensed an anti-intellectual attitude among the indigenous pastors and leaders. They regarded formal theological education as "unspiritual." Since most educational opportunities were offered by Christian ministries from the West, Jewish leaders tended to view this as a foreign imposition. Besides, they were native Hebrew speakers and could read the Bible in its original language!

Experiencing National Growth

Directly, King of Kings Community has given birth to six congregations. Indirectly, several members of King of Kings, after moving to other parts of Israel, have taken the initiative to plant congregations without our official involvement. One couple, who led our King of Kings youth ministry, moved to Haifa and started one of the most extensive and fruitful ministries in Israel. Others who came to faith among us went on to lead ministries in Arabic-speaking and Russian-speaking contexts. Graduates of Israel College of the Bible have gone on to pioneer new congregations, as well.

When we launched King of Kings Community in 1983, our best estimates show that there were about fifteen congregations in Israel. Today, there are more than 200. The Body of Israeli Jewish believers in 1983 was less than 1,000; today, we estimate that it is more than 20,000. We do not claim to be the principal cause of this growth, but in investing in making disciples and training leaders, we have played a catalytic role in this movement.

Of the six churches we've planted, nationals lead four of them. Most of the congregations are messianic Jewish, but we also have an Arabic plant on the way. We now have the small home group and prayer group that we hope will grow into a church. If I were to guess the actual numbers, which we haven't gathered yet, I would say that the demographic breakdown of all six churches is as follows:

- 70 percent of the four congregations are Jewish believers. Some Arab believers are part of these congregations, as well.
- Our larger English gathering, which can have 500-650 people on a Sunday evening, would have maybe 20-25 percent Jewish believers, and maybe 5 percent Arab believers in that context. The rest are internationals.

One way that we contextualize our ministry into this particularly Jewish culture is to go back to the roots of almost every truth that we proclaim when we preach. We go back to the Old Testament, just making the connections so that a Jew who knows some of the Scriptures—and they all learn something, even in primary school—will be able to connect with that common ground. We do this consciously all the time. We're preaching from the New Testament a lot, but always bringing in the Hebrew roots of that teaching.

With so much focus on Israel as God's people in this land, we've had to overcome the challenge of reminding everyone that we're all a part of the global family of God. This is one of the reasons we just established the ministry called Fellowship of Israel Related Ministries (FIRM). Its aim is to connect the global church with the body of Christ in Israel. In fact, at our conference two weeks ago, we had one of our largest spaces dedicated to connecting people at a roundtable. It's a bit like speed dating—15 minutes for a local ministry leader to sit with a pastor or marketplace leader from around the world to just share a little bit of their story and then hope that there will be a follow-up and that a natural bond is developed. So we're consciously doing that. We want the local believers to see the bigger picture—because it's possible to be quite insular. But we're fighting that spirit.

On a similar note, at things like our FIRM-sponsored Jerusalem Encounter Conference, we're talking about the focus not being "Israel." In the whole network of ministries, we're trying to engage the church with what God is doing in Israel. It's about his name and his reputation and his glory. So Israel is not the thing; it's about the God of Israel.

Elements of Success

As a part of this case study, we want to share elements of why we believe we've seen success. It's all by the grace of God, but we hope that by identifying these elements, you'll be able to see them more clearly in other contexts:

- *Long-term Vision.* We came to Israel ready to make this our permanent home and life calling. When most global workers left Israel during the Gulf War in 1991, we stayed. In many ways, our decision to remain in Israel solidified our relationships and trust with the indigenous believers.
- *Prayer Focus.* It has been through prayer that we have received vision and strategy for planting—and prayer has been the engine we've needed to stay the course. We are particularly blessed by the intercessors who pray 16 hours a day in our Jerusalem Prayer Tower.
- *Solid Financial Backing.* Our church-planting effort has been made possible to a considerable degree because of the blessing and financial support of the Pentecostal Assemblies of Canada. This

fellowship of about 1,100 churches sent us out, and they continue to stand solidly behind us. Increasingly, churches and individuals from around the world are partnering with us in the gospel.

- *A Spirit of Unity and Servanthood.* We view King of Kings as a "servant ministry." I have often quoted the motto: "It's amazing what you can accomplish if you don't care who gets the credit." We have opened our substantial facilities for use by the broader body of believers in Jerusalem. When many landlords refused to rent to messianic congregations, we were able to make our spaces available. Of the dozen or so congregations, several of them were planted by King of Kings Ministries.

The unity piece here stands out as we look back at our story. This is true of the unity of our leadership team in particular; it has been amazing. I was part of the team that organized a semi-annual worship and prayer retreat for leaders in the land: both Jewish and Arab, and people like me who came from somewhere else. We've done this for about 20 years. Not all can attend each time. But it's remarkable—the amount of unity we experience. And by the way, our own ministry has expanded beyond just Jewish outreach. We have an Arabic work as well. Our school of media has been primarily both Jews and Arab students, with some internationals. The Bible College that we turned over to the local body has done much better than we could have ever done. It's one-third Arab students and two-thirds Jewish students. That's a real testimony of unity.

Looking Forward

In September 2015, I handed the senior pastor role to our associate pastor, Chad Holland. He is 21 years my junior. I continue, however, to serve as president of King of Kings Ministries (KKM) and remain on the pastoral and executive team, as well as preach every few months. Chad is proving to be an exceptional leader and shares my passion for church planting.

KKM has planted congregations that would remain under the direction of the "mother" congregation for one year and then be released. While there were some benefits to this "throw them in the deep end" approach, most of the congregations would have benefited from more ongoing support and counsel from the leaders of KKM. Chad Holland believes that developing a relational network adds strength to new plants as well as other congregations that would voluntarily join in. Chad has initiated "Sarigim," (Hebrew for "branches," based on John 15:5), an Israel-wide network of congregations.

Over the past year, King of Kings Ministries has launched two congregations simultaneously. One is in the city of Herzliya, the high-tech capital of Israel, located north of Tel Aviv. The other is in Jerusalem, a plant with characteristics of traditional, synagogue-style worship. Both plants have begun with the agreement that they will maintain a close relationship with KKM.

King of Kings Ministries is more passionate than ever to make disciples who make disciples and plant life-giving congregations that will expand God's kingdom in Israel. As I looked forward toward finding a successor, I looked for someone with a business background. I found a man who had a degree in business, but he was also a pastor. And he really has a head for that. So it just comes naturally to him. It's just having the right people to make that happen. Frankly, if I were absorbed continuously in this, I couldn't do anything else. Chad has the gifts for that.

A COMMUNITY-FORWARD APPROACH

St. Jax, Montreal

Graham A. Singh

Archdeacon Linda Borden-Taylor had led the Anglican Diocese of Montreal's flagship church, St. James the Apostle, for some fifteen years. At the center of Canada's second largest city—representing the glory days of anglophone rule over this francophone culture—this heritage building brought both good and ill to the missional opportunity it was charged with stewarding. Over the past ten years, the church had struggled with fewer numbers of increasingly difficult people. The congregation had spent down its endowment of over three million dollars and was hoping to sell its church hall to release another five million of capital available for operational overspend. Although it had attempted a number of innovative parish models, the church understood that it had three years to turn around—or face closure, radical surgery, or both.

Bishop Mary Irwin-Gibson was the new Diocesan Bishop. Having obeyed a sense of God's calling in allowing her name to stand for an election she had lost some ten years earlier, Mary won the election of her peers. She now faced the daunting task of turning around a struggling Diocese of some eighty churches, many of whom felt orphaned as traditional Anglicans surrounded by a hostile secular and francophone culture. Mary also had experience of running fourteen Alpha Courses in a small country parish and had faith for God to do an entirely new thing at the start of her episcopacy. On her first day of pre-briefing for the new role, Mary read a proposal for completely closing and then reopening one of the most challenging churches in the Diocese.

Mark Dunwoody was the Diocesan Missioner, charged with finding new ideas within a church culture that seemed to eat novelty for breakfast. Mark had been a Youth Worker in Northern Ireland during the "Troubles" of the late 1980s and had the sense of humor and passionate heart of prayer to pull together a miraculous plan. Mark went to a national conference of the Anglican Church of Canada, where he met a young Canadian leader who had spent the previous decade reopening closed churches in England.

Some 8,000 churches were closed throughout the UK, leading to a crisis over what to do with these empty buildings.[1] The first church plants were planted in the 1980s, but it was not until the early 2000s that Nicky Gumbel began making national statements to the Church Commissioners in England (the denominational body which governs the alteration and closure of church buildings, among other functions) imploring them to stop closing any more church buildings. "You name the building, we will send a team," said Gumbel one famous Sunday in 2002, and the author of this case and hundreds of others stood up to say "Over our dead bodies too!" Since that time, over fifty closed historic churches have been reopened or planted, in England.

I was an Anglican Priest trained in the Church of England's new school of church planting, St. Mellitus College. Having come alive in my faith at Holy Trinity Brompton (where I also met my wife, Celine, from France), I became part of a new leadership pipeline beginning with Alpha and subsequently received theological education and finally in-context training for Anglican ordination. I had been apprenticed and sent out in two church plants from Holy Trinity Brompton involving teams of fifty people each time, sent to reopen closed historic churches in London. Sensing God's call back to my native land of Canada and having received the sending permission of my UK-based team, my wife, Celine, and I, along with our three children, were now looking for an opportunity to explore the "HTB model of church planting" in the best possible Canadian city-center location.

Linda, Mary, Mark, and I began working on a new plan to bring these four perspectives together. St. James the Apostle was closed and the new church plant of St. Jax Montreal was birthed.

The existing parish was closed on December 31, 2015. This was not the decision of a thriving parish to hand over to something new. It was, rather, the more clinical ending of something which had already been labeled as untenable. Thanks to Diocesan desperation from years gone by, a declaration that "you are in your last three years—or else" had been made by the previous Bishop. This helped bring a sobering reality into certain parts of the congregation which, until then, had fallen prey to the attitude that *this is St. James the Apostle; of course we will always keep going*, and became a very useful text for both the change management and grief elements of the new project. The timing of Bishop Mary's formal closure process of three months was, in fact, the end timing already prescribed in the three-year "final review" process. Bishop Mary's final letter (which can be made available upon request) was not a "request for consultation" but rather a loving announcement, given the desperate and high-stakes nature of the building fabric and congregational health.

STRUCTURE AND STRATEGY

A new church planting process was launched on January 1, 2016 when I was appointed as the new Rector effective that date. I began informal Sunday meetings with members of the former congregation who were interested in finding out about the new venture and mid-week meetings for those who had found out about the plant via social media. By Easter, a new team had been formed and we launched an "HTB-style" Anglican charismatic service on Easter Sunday itself, followed by the running of the Alpha Course on the subsequent Sundays until early summer. During the summer months, small-group Bible studies were started, leading on to a full launch and return to "HTB-style" services in September. In total, the church was closed for nine months of team building and Alpha, during the period between the closure of St. James the Apostle and the full relaunch of St. Jax Montreal. The name "St. Jax Montreal" was created as a new, bilingual short-form combining "James" and "Jacques" and dropping "the Apostle Anglican Church." This rebranding helped communicate some of the other shifts of our vision.

The HTB Model is a result of the explosion of interest in Alpha and subsequent pressures on the growth of the church. Alpha was developed at Holy Trinity Brompton (Diocese of London, Church of England) as a local tool for evangelism in that parish but which generated global interest and was, therefore, developed further into something which could be shared more broadly. Over fifteen sessions, participants receive "teaching not preaching" within an environment of generous hospitality (i.e., great food and a carefully planned welcome) which all lead to a time of totally open discussion. Alpha training is centered around how to not spoil that open discussion with Christian interventions and corrections. From 1977 onwards, interest in Alpha grew at HTB in a way that led to many thousands of people coming to know the Lord Jesus Christ and leading eventually to a shortage of space in that particular parish.

St. Jax Montreal has since developed into a community of some one hundred adults and thirty children meeting on Sundays, as well as a thriving hub of community-based activities. Core community members have come from a wide variety of cultural and church backgrounds, however most are young families who have been reached via social media. Those families tend to have been interested in finding a new church environment which would express an open-minded culture of three stream church (i.e., with spirit, sacrament, and Scripture held in a mission-focused balance). Many new believers have come to faith through Alpha, and we assess the mix of de-churched and un-churched on a daily basis. Community-based activities include rental agreements with the City of Montreal for their downtown free concert series, as well as the charity "Action Refugee Montreal" whose staff of twelve is hosted in the church offices. Events like the United Nations High Commission for Refugees World Refugee Day and National Police Week have also been hosted in this city-center site. This use of the building as a community center has emerged as a key theme over this first year. Throughout this period, three Alpha Courses have been run, each time in two groups of French- and English-speaking participants in two connected rooms. Worship, prayer, building work, and administration have all been developed through the building of team and projects. It is this mix of bilingual evangelistic, discipleship, and community-based events that has given St. Jax its unique flavor.

Looking ahead, St. Jax is developing the Trinity Centre for training of five similar projects from around North America, within a cohort system related to Doctor of Ministry research I did based at Asbury Theological Seminary. Selection for this learning cohort will be based on three criteria:

1. Outstanding city-center historic church building
2. Exceptional, experienced and godly leadership with skills in management
3. A well-protected blank slate for innovation within a historic denomination

It is hoped that the Doctorate of Ministry major project will be wrapped around the creation of the training program required for this cohort.

CHALLENGES

Resistance to Change

The Anglican Diocese of Montreal is typical of North American Anglicanism because its liturgical and cultural history offers a spiritual orthodoxy but social liberalism. Almost all of the eighty churches of the Diocese are anglophone and expressing a culture of a much older English generation. If it might be said that there are a dozen major forms of Anglicanism, globally speaking, it could be argued that only two or three of those forms existed within the Diocese of Montreal. The argument for experimenting with one of those as-yet-unused forms (the "HTB model") was a key strand of the logic behind allowing the St. Jax experiment. The high rate and threat of church closures created an environment of fear in which new innovation has on a number of occasions been resisted, yet alongside this has come a deep desperation for change. Bishop Mary Irwin-Gibson has led the clarion call to try something new, and the positive response from the Diocese has been deeply humbling for all concerned. It is within this mix of emotions that God can be seen to be particularly at work in his mission of unity, reformation, and revival.

A Bilingual Environment

The typical language of Downtown Montreal is a lightly bilingual "franglais," yet the vast majority of churches are either 100 percent French or 100 percent English, as is the case in our Anglican Diocese. This has been a huge obstacle for the development of Anglicanism in this region but may also have sped along a helpful journey to desperation. From this stage of desperation all "sacred cows" can be either slain (or penned) in order to allow innovation to occur. We serve a "Dead Alive God" who did not hide in a cave for three days but rather was both crucified and resurrected. We know what it means to be "Dead Alive People" as we die to ourselves and live only for Christ. What we have yet to learn is how to respond to "Dead Alive Churches" which cannot be rebooted but rather need to totally close and die in order to sufficiently innovate. In the case of Montreal, it is Quebec's bilingual culture that has helped the Diocese understand its own imminent death in a more realistic way.

The "Quiet Revolution"

Not only is there a linguistic challenge but also a socio-political one from the forty-year phenomenon known in Quebec as "The Quiet Revolution."[2] During this political change orchestrated by the Quebec Premier (Provincial Leader), Renee Levesque, three significant moves were made by all of *Québécois* culture. The first is against all anglophones, in protest of their colonizing influence in language and economy. The second is against all other forms of colonialism, including any aspect of European culture. The third turning is against the Catholic Church and any other Christian voice with similar content. For example, it is both impossible and illegal for a wife to take the family name of her husband. In reflecting on the Quiet Revolution in the wider Western world, it might be said that these three turnings are in fact present in many other societies. Perhaps the Quiet Revolution is a "Ghost of Christmas Future" for others? In the case of St. Jax Montreal and its Anglican Diocese, moves like opening a bilingual French/English service and Alpha, having a female Bishop, and a less combative response to questions of human sexuality, have become important antidotes and missional openings to the challenge of the Quiet Revolution.

A Large, Costly Building

The building of St. James the Apostle—recall that St. Jax Montreal is the bilingual short name, but the former building name remains—is a 150-year old stone building with a slate roof. The estimated repair cost for the basic fabric of the building is five million dollars, and this work is urgently required. This challenge has been greatly helped by the tragic sale of other church buildings in the Diocese, as well as a willingness to use the building primarily as a community center and secondarily as a church. A full-time Operations Director was employed from the earliest days of the plant, to recognize the challenge and opportunity of running this site.

Recruiting a New Church-Planting Team Without a Mother Church

This challenge could have been much worse. One theory was that large church-planting teams were the human product of a well-organized church at Holy Trinity Brompton. Another theory is that God will send the team he needs, wherever he so desires. The St. Jax experience has shown that God has been more than able to mobilize a team of gifted, experienced, and teachable Christians, even without the local presence of a mother church, as in the London-based instances of the HTB model.

RESPONSE

It was hoped that a "suitcase full of church-planting tools," as it were, from Holy Trinity Brompton would be of some use in Montreal. The basic methodology was to unpack this suitcase and see which British tools fit this new Canadian context. In general, the response to this theory has been beyond what we expected, or in other words, all of these various tools seem to be working thus far. The process of firmly closing the church, rather than attempting a church growth methodology, was shown to have clear benefits in the change-management process. The Alpha Course was found to be highly effective in streamlining the theological assumptions of the new planting team, as well as focusing the team on a form of relational evangelism at the core of this new discipleship model. An early decision to reposition the church first as a community center and second as a church has helped break through major local political challenges of "The Quiet Revolution."

Congregation vs. Planting Team

One of the many tensions in the St. Jax response has been between the planting of a congregation and the building of a planting team. In the case of a congregation, the emphasis is on providing activities, services, and features of church life which attract and grow a group of faithful worshippers. If a person came to see what the preaching was like, for instance, they would be deciding about joining an environment where the features were to their liking. Aspects of teaching on Alpha, for instance, or of the musical worship, could be assessed to be more or less suited to a particular person or family.

In the case of the development of a church-planting team, the criteria are significantly different. The idea of selecting appropriate team members based on God's supernatural calling, spiritual maturity, agreement with vision, availability of time, willingness to give—these might help the leadership of such a team decide whether that person was an appropriate member of the church-planting team, or whether they and the church might be better served in another environment. St. Jax has been an example of the development of a planting team and not a congregation, and this has been evidenced in the several occasions in which inappropriate team members have been gently asked to leave in order to ensure a healthy early team.

Reasons for deeming someone less suitable, for instance, might be around issues of male/female headship or prayer-ministry models. In one case, a team member regularly criticized our Diocesan Bishop (based in her gender) and also asked every new person if they were "born again." After attempting several failed attempts to underline the importance of episcopal authority and more restraint in conversation, the person in question was asked to leave the team. There are a number of other examples, which are more difficult to share in this report!

The result of this careful work has been to create a much higher degree of unity. It is our belief that this unity is a carrier of blessing and has been hugely helpful in the subsequent stages of growth, which inevitably will begin to look increasingly congregational.

Three Stream vs. Sacramental, Evangelical, or Charismatic

The idea of holding evangelical, sacramental, and charismatic in harmony has been key to the development of St. Jax. In the HTB model, this unique blend of Anglicanism and the charismatic movement, exemplified by John Wimber (and others), has become part of the national fabric of much of the Church of England. In the Anglican Church of Canada, this same blend has been strongly resisted. From its inception, St. Jax has used a "three stream operating system" wherein sacramental traditions of the Eucharist and lectionary, charismatic practices of prayer ministry in the laying on of hands, and Evangelical models of clear and open teaching and discussion can all sit together. This mix has been very well received in Downtown Montreal, where some people call this "hipster."

Community Center vs. Church

Many thriving urban center churches develop significant community and care ministries. In the St. Jax case, several community activities were already present and kept active, even through the closing of the church congregation. Most aspects of this reality were positive, including the presence of a large refugee resettlement charity, the regular and thriving meetings of Alcoholics Anonymous, and the City of Montreal's concert series on Saturday nights. This experience of church planting has helped the team to ask, "What if we weren't running a church at all but simply a community center—how much favor with the community would we experience?" The assumed answer is that the favor gained from this offering is very great indeed. The challenge for this team has been to carefully layer on a new worshipping and evangelistic community without disturbing the benefits of this already-established local impact.

The first instance of this challenge occurred with a homeless center located in the basement of the church whose owners refused to sign a new lease obligating them to take part in the Diocesan safe church policy. Over several previous years, behavior on the margins of the homeless center had become increasingly worse, such that it had significantly impacted all other activities in the church for vulnerable adults, young families, and children. Hypodermic needles, feces, and other garbage had become a chronic nightly problem and this particular community tenant's management board had become particularly numb to the problem. In the end, the center chose to leave the church within a negative media storm. This also became a formational moment for the community center concept at St. Jax.

Since that time, a much more carefully planned concept has evolved. This includes the description of "missional subsidies" wherein charitable and Christian groups can be offered a discount, in favor of their contribution or compatibility to the vision of the church. In other words, any discount needs to be justified based on excellent and collaborative community impact. This sits within a broader concept of "cost centers" in the church financial structures, where church, community center, capital project, and training centers each have distinct income, expenditure, and sharing of costs, including running and staff costs. For instance, some 80,000 dollars of the 450,000-dollar operating budget is assigned to the capital project, in light of the huge toll on staff and the building that construction management requires.

These various strands of thinking have helped the St. Jax team to carefully manage the responsibilities of the huge building that they occupy. One result has been a detailed letter of support from the Mayor of Montreal, a 200,000-dollar grant from the Quebec government, and vastly improved relationship with building tenants and neighbors. This structure has even allowed for the building to be shared by three other church groups. By sharing the building in a more intentional way, it may be said that a better long-term future is being developed than other common models of "we'll pay the bills and you chip in a little."

Diocese-led vs. Diocese-influenced

St. Jax Montreal's most senior leadership team has a monthly meeting of Rector, Bishop, Archdeacon and Diocesan Missioner, many of whom—but not all, all of the time—are also present in regular Sunday worship. The active leadership team has a staff meeting on Tuesday mornings. By keeping the Diocesan team very close to the running of the church, the subtle intricacies of the HTB model can be explored and shared in both broad and fine levels of detail in a way which can bring wider positive change to the Diocese. By agreeing on a clear strategic path and timeline in conjunction with the Diocese of London, the risk of drifting or being dragged out of focus by the Diocese of Montreal is low. The opportunity for great discussion and integration with other Diocesan themes is high. This is a theme taken from the HTB model but extended and enhanced in this unique Montreal situation.

Movemental vs. Local

The vision of Holy Trinity Brompton is "to play our part in the re-evangelization of the nations, the revitalization of the church and the transformation of society,"[3] and the adoption of this wider vision in Montreal has helped the St. Jax team to focus on its outward impact, right from the start. As was seen at HTB itself, this outward and movemental focus has in fact attracted some of the most capable and godly local leaders and kept the team focused on Alpha, prayer, and worship in an effective way.

REFLECTION

This case study is unfolding as we speak and reflections here are early. In general, it seems as though the HTB model does indeed "work" as a City Centre Resource Church model, even with HTB itself not present as the mother church. Hundreds of people have participated in Alpha and Sunday worship. Hundreds more have attended special events and seasonal festivals. Thousands of "community contact hours" have taken place already through secular use of the building. The idea of community center and church in a new kind of harmony has also been surprisingly effective and fruitful.

One of the major risks in this situation was the perceived danger in connecting what is seen as part of the "evangelical" side of the Anglican Church into what is perceived as a "liberal" Diocese. It may be proposed that both of those categories are insufficient and, in fact, this danger has been turned into a beautiful kingdom opportunity for peacemaking. Quebec is a very socially liberal society, and a socially conservative evangelistic outreach would be destroyed before it started. This is evidenced by the radical decline of evangelical outreach in other parts of the church. By avoiding this bombastic approach to the City, far greater opportunities for evangelism have been presented and the best of those have been in response to other community partnerships. The willingness to build this church plant on an unrelenting commitment to reaching the culture has, in fact, opened up orthodox missional opportunities (preaching/leading/social ethics/community building)—beyond the team's wildest imagination.

Looking ahead, the challenge of sustaining growth will no doubt be a theme for every aspect of church life. Financial pressures of a large capital project, along with a movemental imperative to share our learning, all connect together in pressure on team and resources.

The importance of earnest and regular corporate prayer has perhaps slipped due to the challenges of gathering young families. We want to make Sunday mornings truly superior to midweek meetings. The importance of being willing to go back and correct early mistakes or smooth out ruffled feathers will be seen in this stage of the next two to five years. Other denominational pressures, changes of leadership, and unexpected situations pose a certain risk to stability. However, even despite those concerns and known risks, the future for St. Jax is a hopeful one, and it is great blessing to share this story and to invite the prayers of all readers! We thank God for the beautiful opportunity to serve him in this way and pray that his will would continue to be done, on earth as it is in heaven.

MINISTERING IN THE MARGINS

Christian Evangelistic Assemblies, India

John Varghese & Varghese Samuel

ev. Dr. George Chavanikamannil founded the Christian Evangelistic Assemblies and dedicated his life for the ministry in North India. His passion was to reach unreached people at any cost. Early on in his life, he realized the need of "taking the whole gospel" to the whole people of India. With this vision, along with his energy and resources, George realized that it would not be possible to achieve this goal alone. He came up with a calculation that if a person preaches the gospel to 1,000 different people a day, 365 days a year, it would take 2739.72 years to reach 1 billion people. The impossibility of such a task made him realize the need to equip thousands of ministers to preach the gospel. Training as many people as possible seemed to be the only way to reach all of India. The Scripture says, "The harvest is plenteous but the laborers are few..." (Matt. 9:37).

Another driving force behind the inception of the CEA is the Great Commission of the Lord. The Lord Jesus commanded, "Go and make disciples of all nations" (*ethna*, *Jati*, or "people groups," Matt. 28:19). India has 4,963 people groups, probably one of the largest varieties of ethnic groups in one nation in the world.[1] Many of them are spread throughout the central and northern states of India. Hundreds of them have not yet been reached with the gospel. The tribal communities in India are apprehensive about people and cultures from outside and are unwilling to listen to and accept them unless this distrust is broken and their trust gained. In this context, taking the gospel as an outsider is not an easy task.

The only feasible alternative is to train their own people who have responded to the gospel and send them back to win their kinsmen. As a primary step into the ministry in North India, George founded Bharat Susamachar Samiti (BSS) in Dehra Dun in North India in 1986. Under this parent body, Luther W. New Jr. Theological College, popularly known as New Theological College, was founded in 1987. The training of ministers started in 1987, when many students from different states and tribes of India joined the short-term courses in the early years of the college. As the students received training, they were also challenged to take the gospel to the unreached places in India. Consequently, several of them ventured into semi-urban and rural areas and planted small congregations. Pastors of these congregations came together for fellowship and prayer and attracted a few likeminded pastors, who joined the fellowship.

As the number of fellowship gatherings grew and spread through different nearby states, it became necessary to have a formal organization of churches to function well and to fulfill the vision and mission of the founder. New ministries were started in a few places in three states of India (Uttar Pradesh, Madhya Pradesh and Orissa), and a few congregations were established. It was in 1992 that the ministry was formalized and Christian Evangelistic Assemblies was officially formed. The founder, Rev. Dr. George Chavanikamannil, along with a few leaders who were working with him at that time, called the first meeting of the leaders of Christian Evangelistic Assemblies.

STRUCTURE AND STRATEGY

The first meeting of the Board of Directors of Christian Evangelistic Assemblies was held on Tuesday, June 19th, 1992, on the premises of New Theological College. In this meeting, important decisions were taken as to the future direction, functioning, and structure of the church. Some of the decisions that actually shaped the course of action to achieve the vision and goals of the organization included: the decision to expand to all the states of India with national registration, to work in teams going to new places where the gospel had not been preached, and to appoint ministers at three different levels (recognized, licensed, and ordained). Thus, the informal ministry took on the form of an organized church.

These decisions provided enough enthusiasm to encourage the members to press on toward the goal. Yet much work remained to be done. The CEA realized the need to train and equip young men and women to work in the villages and towns in North India. Several young men and women had been trained in New Theological College, and depending on the need and complexity of the ministry, they were trained either for one year or four years. Many of them have now gone to other places and established churches. As the ministry expanded to cover more than ten Indian states, it became necessary to further organize the ministry's structure to be more effective. Hence, the churches in different states were brought under regional organizations. In 1993, the ministry was segregated into three regions—the Northern, North Eastern and Central regions.

Later, these regions were further expanded to include seven additional regions:

1. Arunachal and Assam
2. Bihar and Jharkhand
3. Orissa and Andhra Pradesh
4. Madhya Pradesh, Maharashtra, and Chhattisgarh
5. Delhi and Haryana
6. Uttar Pradesh and Uttarakhand
7. Punjab and Himachal Pradesh

Coordinators were assigned to oversee these ministries and meet with the pastors regularly, once a month. To make the work even better coordinated and more effective, the ministers in every team gather together every month to discuss strategy, pray together, listen to others, and have fellowship. It is mandatory for every minister to be part of a team, as it was found that members of a team performed better than those who worked independently. The reason is that they receive better support, guidance, and necessary help in times of need.

The vision of the CEA is to see people "from every nation, tribe, people and language" (Rev. 7:9) worshipping the Lord Jesus Christ in heaven and to plant churches in places where there are no churches already. Since India is a land of myriad tribes, languages, and people groups (*ethne* in Greek), a Christian presence and the number of churches is minimal throughout the North Indian belt. Reaching this area of India with the gospel is the greatest challenge before the Indian church. The Christian Evangelistic Assemblies is committed to see this vision fulfilled. The focus of the ministry is primarily among the poor, downtrodden, neglected, marginalized, and the outcasts of the mainstream of society. However, we also minister to people of all levels of society with a goal to transform their lives—morally, ethically, and spiritually—through kingdom principles and values. To achieve these goals, several methods are adopted with the understanding that preaching the gospel alone is not sufficient for holistic transformation. It is also important to care for the needs of people, educate them in order to help them discover their potential, and make them aware of their rights, as well as to give them enough support for self-sustenance. The aims and objectives of the Christian Evangelistic Assemblies are to be actively involved in the mission of the church based on the foundation of the New Testament Church.

Though reflection of our success story is not the main intention of this paper, let me highlight a few achievements we have received because of God's faithfulness towards us. CEA has been ministering in the semi-urban and rural areas of the fourteen states of India for over two decades. We were able to achieve the following during this time. CEA was able to take the gospel to many places where the gospel has not reached and to many people who have not heard. Several churches were established. We have approximately 450 churches in fourteen states. If we take an average of fifty baptized people in a congregation, the total number of baptized believers among these churches is 22,500. But there are many more that come for worship who are not baptized. More than 300 grassroots-level Christian workers were trained over a period of six years. Apart from that more than 1,000 graduates have passed out from Luther W. New Jr. Theological College with Bachelor's and Master's degrees. Many of their lives were drastically changed, and in turn, they are trying to bring transformation in their own society and among their people. Most of them are working as church planters. Presently, there are seven satellite-training centers. We are able to care for many poor and needy children through three children's homes. Five academic schools at the primary level are functioning. Christian Evangelistic Assemblies has been able to bring social and economic transformation, besides spiritual transformation, in the lives of many people who came to faith through our ministries. People have started thinking about living a dignified life with aim and purpose. They want to send their children to school and lead a decent life. They are also delivered from superstitions and many bad habits. Economically, many of them have made progress and have a desire to save money for the future, contrary to what they have been practicing. There are ample opportunities to bring transformation—socially, economically, academically, and spiritually—in the lives of people who are sidelined from the mainstream of the society.

CHALLENGES

Christian Evangelistic Assemblies has worked in mainly rural areas, planting around 450 churches, the same churches I cited above. During the course of our ministry, we have faced several challenges and difficulties. The rest of this paper attempts to focus on the challenges (with opportunities) that the CEA has faced, especially the challenges faced by people who are unable to profess their Christian faith openly.

Caste Feelings

Caste feelings play a major role in the Indian mind, and it cripples the message of the gospel. Many people come to Christianity hoping for better acceptance from the neglect they have faced in the Hindu society for centuries. But the irony is that they bring the caste feelings with them to church. Many people know the truth, but when it comes to associating with people of other castes, especially with lower castes, they are unable to do so. This has greatly hindered our work.

Most of our congregations are house churches, which has its advantages and disadvantages. In Indian societies, especially in North India, as the caste system is very strong, people from different castes and people groups find it difficult to gather for worship in the house of a person from a different caste, especially if that person is from a lower caste. Hence, people hesitate to come together for worship in house churches, though the situation has slightly improved. But if the worship is held in a common place, the problem is largely solved.

Marriages

Finding suitable partners for adult children is very important for parents. The people who come to our churches are first-generation Christians. When they leave the community they have been a part for generations to join a minority community, finding partners for their sons and daughters is a major issue! Many people, though they want to come out and profess Christ as their Lord and Savior, back out because they're thinking about the future of their children. Our society is not kind to unmarried people, especially to women. So the parents cannot think about seeing their children remaining unmarried. For the first-generation Christians, it often feels almost impossible to find a suitable match. Many times, the church is also unable to help the new believers. To profess Christian faith brings uncertain futures for young people. For this reason, many people don't come to church.

Social Alienation and Ostracism

This is another major problem that new believers face in India. As soon as they come to Christian faith, many are accused of rejecting their traditional *dharam* (religion) and gods and goddesses. Usually, the *Panchayat* (a village court) is called and the "infidels" are tried. They put a ban on several things for such individuals—such as prohibiting purchasing groceries from the local stores and public distribution shops, prohibiting them from taking water from the public well so they cannot drink it, nor can they use it for their cattle and fields; they may also not allow them to participate in public and social events like marriages, deaths, and festivals, etc. These kinds of discrimination and alienation are very taxing on social life, and many times, people look down at them with hatred and hostility. Only very few people have the boldness to stand up against such alienation.

Education of Children

Educating children is one of the major challenges faced by our new believers. Most of our ministries are in rural areas, where there are very few schools—and government-run schools at that. In these schools, every morning, the students are expected to bow down before the idol of a deity and sing "Saraswati Vandana," which is a mantra connected to idol worship. The children of new believers find it very difficult to figure out the best educational setting as we teach very strongly against idol worship. The children have no option whether or not to sing. A few parents revealed that they ask their church wards that they may do it for the sake of the authorities and to stay in school. If they do not do it, their children will be expelled from the school. There are no Christian schools, and the parents cannot afford to send their kids to far-off schools. Even a few of our evangelists did not send their children to school for a period of time. Many parents do not want to risk the education of their children. Hence, they compromise and do not profess their faith. Also, during the festivals each student has to give a small donation in cash for festival celebrations, as well as rituals during festivals in the temples. Denying the donation will result in expulsion of that student from the school. This is mainly seen among our Bihar fellowships.

Benefits from the Government

People belonging to lower castes receive certain grants, allowances, helps, scholarships, and subsidies from the government. But as soon as they become Christians, these benefits cease. We have several examples of people whose ration cards are cancelled just because they became Christians. Any amount of coaxing and pleading would do no good in these cases as the neighbors and villagers are bent on making the lives of new believers miserable.

As a result, many people maintain a dual identity. When they come to the church, they are Christians, but in government records they are listed as Hindus. However, many are unwilling to keep this dual status. They are simply unwilling to profess their Christian faith for fear of losing benefits from the government. I have personal experiences of talking to such people who say, *"Are' saab, hum to balbache wale hai. Agar yeh bhi nahi milta hai to hum bhooke marenge."* This is translated, "Sir, we have kids and our wife to feed. If we don't get these benefits we will perish in our hunger." If we put ourselves in their shoes, we will not be able to condemn them.

Giving chanda (donations)

In the rural areas giving *chanda* (donations) for festivals and *pujas* is an important factor of social interdependence and unity. However, because of strong teachings in the church against being part of idol worship, many new believers refuse to give *chanda* and join such activities. They are persecuted and many times ostracized from the society. It becomes impossible for them to live in the community. Many of them give up and say, "*Hum jante hai ki yeh galat hain. Par hum kya karen, hame jeene nahi dete,*" which means "We know giving such donations are wrong, but if we don't give, life will become hell for us."

The truth is that these people, who are pulled between the biblical truth and the social demands, are poor in various senses of the term. Society criticizes, condemns, and alienates them by accusing them of rejecting the traditional religion, gods, and goddesses. At the same time, the church does not fully accept them as true believers because of their seeming indecisiveness.

CEA's View on Social Pressure

CEA has always been sympathetic to such people who are unable to profess their faith openly. Condemning them will not produce any positive result in winning them for Christ. Realizing their difficulty, encouraging them to continue to believe in Christ, sympathetically helping and standing with them can win them at a later time. We have helped several such people through our projects in times of difficulty and encouraged their children in their studies. They remained very friendly and cooperative, even though they never came for worship or any other religious activities.

However, some of our pastors are very conventional in their outlook and prohibit such people from associating with the church in any way. We slowly try to educate them to be sympathetic to them as Jesus and Elisha did, hoping that one day they or their children will profess Christian faith.

Struggling Pastors and Families

As we read in Ephesians 6, "For our struggle is not against flesh and blood, but against the rulers, against the authorities, against the powers of this dark world and against the spiritual forces of evil" (v. 12). Repeatedly, we have seen that pastors and their families go through different kinds of sickness, depression, failures, and deaths, for example, for which they have no reason. This is mainly because of the kind of work that they are involved in. On one hand, the story is bright, but on the other hand, it's a candle burning bright by giving away all that it has to fuel the flame. This is exactly the life of a pastor/missionary/evangelist and their family.

Tithing to and giving for the Lord is difficult to teach the first-generation believers. The responsibility of funding for the church remains on the shoulders of the pastor. He has to support his own family, as well as the church, with limited funds. Lack of finances forces pastors to struggle greatly to provide for the needs of the family, good education for children, weddings for their children, etc. This is solved only when each believer gives honestly for the kingdom of God.

Difficulty in Securing Church Space

India is a religious country, and the place of worship has a lot of significance. Due to lack of places of worship, we have to rent buildings. Any time the owner of the building tells the pastor to vacate, especially if the owner is pressured by the society to remove us, is difficult. The owner also receives pressure from others if anyone from his own family or caste receives Jesus. Moving from one location to another also stagnates growth. For some the worship place will be far off, and they are not be able to come for fellowship.

Lack of Committed People to Work in Unreached Places

With the rise in theology students, seldom do people, after having completed their Bachelor's or Master's or Doctoral studies, turn around and work in a village. Such people would work in a para-church organization or an NGO or want to teach in Bible college and stay within their zone.

Even if such people wish to go to the villages, they first want to know the salary package before they even envision their work. Academic study is necessary, but most of the academic knowledge that we receive in Bible school cannot be applied in the villages where people are illiterate. They must first become literate so they can read the Bible. Unless that happens, we cannot do exegetical preaching among such people. Moreover, pursuing academic education also tempts a person to keep moving further down that path, reducing his age of effectiveness to a few years. For example, if a person goes into a village at the age of twenty-five to make Christ known in that village, he will be able to work for at least fifteen to twenty years tirelessly before age catches up on him. But if that same person spends forty years of his life doing doctoral studies, how many years will they be able to spend in the mission field? Even if he goes, he will be not effective.

Lack of Visionary Missionaries

We talk about the holistic development of the church, but CEA has been able to focus only on spiritual development. We have not been able to run hospitals, schools, and other income-generating activities, let alone concessional service for the poor and marginalized of the society. If this side of the coin is also looked into and proper social services are provided, then we can expect more effective results.

CONCLUSION

In conclusion, let me say that a lot of work has yet to be done in India. Just like our Lord Jesus told his disciples, " The harvest is plentiful but the workers are few" (Matt. 9:37). That same verse can be used in the context of India even today. We need not pray for the harvest; we need to pray for workers. Fasting and praying is the key to winning souls, as well as winning India for Christ.

FROM THE ENDS OF THE EARTH

Mission China 2030, China

Paul Chang

The Chinese church surprised the global church in the latter part of the 20th century. Since communitarianism, the Chinese church has produced remarkable revival in the form of the house church without the help of overseas churches. The revival of the Chinese Club is comparable to the history of the early church, and it is difficult to reasonably explain it without the work of the Holy Spirit.

The Chinese church shows another unique phenomenon: most Chinese Christians share a common moral vision. The common vision is called "Back to Jerusalem Movement" (a.k.a., BTJ Movement). The vision was birthed among Chinese Christians during the 1920s. Back to Jerusalem is the goal of the Chinese church to evangelize the unreached peoples starting from eastern provinces of China, moving westward toward Jerusalem.[1] Since that time, the clubs of China have striven, and even suffered persecution, to fulfill what they believe is their integral role in fulfilling the Great Commission. The church of China not only evangelizes the religiously oppressed areas of Asia but also trains and sends Chinese missionaries into the unreached regions of the globe, including Muslim, Buddhist, and Hindu nations.

Since the 1990s, various agencies and church leaders, such as Rev. Thomas Wang and Brother Yun, have tried to mobilize BTJ Movement to achieve the vision. However, it has failed to produce remarkable results due to various factors. From 1920 until now, the churches of China have not achieved the BTJ vision, but they still believe that the vision came from God to them.

THE BELT AND ROAD INITIATIVE

Since the 1980s, China has achieved remarkable economic growth. Until 2015, China was the world's fastest-growing major economy, with growth rates averaging 10 percent over thirty years. China has developed into the second largest economy (after the United States) with its GDP reaching 11.2 trillion USD.[2]

After completing the domestic economic growth stage, Xi Jinping, the Chinese leader, announced a drastic foreign economic development plan, which is known as the "Belt and Road Initiative," for faster economic growth and foreign development. The Belt and Road Initiative focuses on connectivity and cooperation between Eurasian countries, primarily the People's Republic of China, India, Central Asia, Russia, Southeast Asia, and middle eastern countries. It is vast, encompassing countries that account for 29 percent of the GDP. Estimates indicate that Belt and Road infrastructure projects in Asia alone will require investments of 1.7 trillion USD per year through to 2030. Currently 900 projects are planned (or are underway), benefitting more than eighty countries. It will invest 25 trillion USD in eastern Asia, Southeast Asia, Central Asia, India, Arabia, Russia, and Europe until 2050. China's Belt and Road Initiative is creating enormous business opportunities throughout Asia, Africa, and Europe. The Belt and Road Initiative will change 4.5 billion people's lives whose areas are undeveloped.[3] The Belt and Road Initiative will provide an incredible opportunity for the Chinese Church to fulfill its BTJ vision. As the past gospel was transmitted from the west to the east of the Eurasian continent through the silk road, the Belt and Road Initiative will provide a huge opportunity for the gospel to be delivered to the undeveloped areas of the Eurasian continent by the Chinese church.

ABOUT MISSION CHINA 2030

So far, I have presented two elements of the background of the BTJ Movement: First, the Chinese Church had a strong and common vision—BTJ. However, the Chinese Church has failed to achieve the vision. Second, the Belt and Road Initiative opens a new door to complete the BTJ vision through the Chinese Club. In this situation, the Chinese Church needs a new missional movement to complete the BTJ vision. So the Chinese Church has initiated the Mission China 2030 movement (a.k.a., MC 2030).

The MC 2030 was proposed by Daniel Jin, who is a prominent leader of the Chinese Club, in the 2013 Seoul Summit. The Seoul Summit was held by the Lausanne Committee and the Chinese Church. In his speech at this summit, Jin suggested for the Chinese Church to send out 20,000 missionaries to cross-cultural areas until 2030. He reported that approximately 20,000 foreign missionaries have come and served Chinese Christians since Robert Morrison came to China in 1807. Therefore, he encourages the Chinese Club to pay back the debt of the gospel to foreign clubs and obey God's calling for mission by sending out 20,000 Chinese missionaries.[4] Hundreds of Chinese and foreign leaders attending the summit officially accepted the proposal of the "Mission China 2030" and decided to promote it as a coalition movement of the Chinese Church.

In recent history, the Chinese Church has not been able to pay much attention to cross-cultural mission because they have to focus on their survival and how to keep their faith. However, the MC 2030 Movement has played a role for the Chinese Church to open up its eyes to global mission again. The MC 2030 movement is awakening them to obey the BTJ vision and share the gospel as far as Jerusalem. The Chinese Church, estimated to be 80 million Christians or more, will be a great force in global mission, when it is awakened and when it joins the global mission by the MC 2030 movement. Considering China's rapid development and increasing importance, the MC 2030 can be a major mission movement representing the non-Western world.

STRUCTURE AND STRATEGY

Implementing the MC 2030 Movement

The MC 2030 movement has its firm organizational structure. Its organizational structure shows the strategies and directions of the movement. MC 2030 starts with five subcommittees: MC0 (Theology and Strategy), MC1 (Domestic Mission), MC2 (Diaspora Mission), MC3 (Ethnic Group Mission), and MC4 (Cross-cultural Mission).

First, the MC0 takes charge of the theology and strategy of the movement. Core leaders of the movement attend the MC0 and determine the overall direction of the movement through discussions of members. The MC1 takes charge of the domestic mission of China. Especially, due to rapid urbanization and social changes of China, it develops urban mission strategy and church-planting ministry within Chinese society. The MC2 takes charge of the Chinese diaspora ministry. There are approximately 60 million overseas Chinese Christians in diaspora all over the world.[5] Because they have diverse cultural backgrounds, special strategies are needed. The MC2 researches and develops mission strategy and mission mobilization strategy for the Chinese diaspora. The MC3 takes charge of minor ethnic-group mission. According to the government, there are fifty-six ethnic minority groups in China except the Han Chinese people, which refers to Korean-speaking Chinese persons. They have their own languages and cultures. MC3 leaders discuss and develop cultural and mission strategies for ethnic groups. Finally, the MC4 takes charge of cross-cultural mission. This division takes charge of researching cultures and targeting areas such as Buddhism, Hinduism, Islam, and folk religions. The MC4 aims to recruit, train, and send out cross-cultural missionaries abroad.

In 2017, the MC 2030 leaders established two new subcommittees: MCY (MC Youth) and MCB (MC Business). MCY is established for the youth and student ministry element of the movement for the continuous development of the Chinese Church. MCB (MC Business) is created to develop business-mission models for Chinese Christian business leaders. Each subcommittee holds its conference once a year and develops its strategies and executes the ministry. The structure of subcommittee shows that the MC 2030 is a very strategic movement. Through its effective development of each of the subcommittees, Chinese churches will be developed strategically in every area.

Annual Conference and Fruits

The MC 2030 movement has a large annual conference outside the country. Until now, they've held three conferences in Hong-Kong, Jeju, and Qiangmai. Each conference has around 1,000 or more in attendance. It is definitely not easy to gather thousands of participants outside of China. However, they conduct it overseas to ensure the safety of the conference. Each conference is held by a regional-church gathering of China such as

Shanghai and Beijing. The annual conference has played a pivotal role in the formation and development of the MC 2030 movement.

The first conference held in Hong Kong was in October 2015. It was hosted by the Shanghai Church Unit. Shanghai All Nations Mission Church and Senior Pastor, Chui Quan, made a great sacrifice to hold the first conference. More than 900 people attended the conference from home and abroad. Between 70 and 80 percent of attendants were church leaders from China. Through this conference, the Chinese church has received the historic call to join God's mission. Chinese domestic leaders and overseas mission leaders gathered and set the common vision and theological foundation of the Mission China 2030 movement. In this conference, Missionary Declaration and Nine Action Guidelines for the MC 2030 were made.

The second meeting was held in Jeju in October 2016. The Beijing Church Unit hosted the conference, and Ezra Jin served the conference as the chairman. In the second conference, strategies and structures were formed to embody the vision of the movement.

The five subcommittees (MC0-MC4) which I described above and their committee members were determined at this event. One of features of the second conference is passionate response and participation of many global mission agencies. Most major mission organizations gathered under the banner of "advisory meeting" with the leadership of the Lausanne committee to support this movement. Overall, the vision of the MC 2030 took shape through the formation of structure and the gathering of more attendees at the Jeju conference.

The third conference was held in Chiang Mai, Thailand, in August 2017. Professor Fang, who has been serving the student ministry for a long time, served the conference as the chairman, and the Rainbow Shanghai Student Association hosted the conference. In order to send out 20,000 missionaries, it was necessary to rise up a student mission movement. So the third conference was held by the youth and designed for the youth. One-third of the 1,200 attendees were college students, and another third were young Christians in their late 20s and early 30s. It seemed like the start of the SVM (Student Volunteer Movement) but as a Chinese version. On the last day, 230 young Chinese Christians responded to God's calling and devoted their lives to God's mission. This conference emphasized calling and training young people for cross-cultural mission, and at the same time strengthened the Chinese campus ministry and student ministry for the Chinese church. This was an important decision for the continuity of the MC 2030 movement and the continuing development of the Chinese church.

Partnership with the Lausanne Movement

The MC 2030 movement has a partnership with the Lausanne Movement. The Lausanne movement provides the basis for the union movement to the Chinese Church through providing evangelical theological background. It is not easy for Chinese Christian leaders to unite and work together in one mind. There are many reasons to prevent united ministry such as regional differences, theological differences, and different traditions. However, the Lausanne movement has offset these differences and has encouraged them to unite and work together.

Further, global mission agencies can participate in the MC movement as partners through the Lausanne Movement. The Lausanne Movement acts as a bridge between MC 2030 and global mission agencies. Until now, 30 to 40 global organizations have joined with deep interest in the movement. The Lausanne informs overseas organizations about the inner situation of Chinese churches, so they can help without misunderstanding. The Chinese Church will be an important partner to the global mission through the MC movement in the future, which is their wish.

CHALLENGES

Maintaining Unity

Maintaining unity is the most important part of the success of the movement. It is inner division, rather than outer resistance, that will distinguish the success or failure of MC 2030. Chinese churches are large and diverse. Currently, eight core leaders are leading this movement. There were many obstacles and long processes that led to the formation of eight leaders among the Chinese churches. Even after the election of eight leaders, the risk of division still exists. They have different theological, cultural, and traditional backgrounds. When they decide the direction and strategy of the movement, they often struggle with different ideas. But so far, leaders of the movement have kept their unity in Christ through prayer and discussion. As I mentioned, keeping this unity in Christ is the most important factor for the success of the movement.

Legal Status and Religious Freedom

Chinese house churches still do not have legal status from the government, so they are not registered with the government. This means that they are subject to many legal and social restrictions. But compared to the old situation in the sixties and seventies, their religious freedom is definitely expanding. However, they still cannot purchase buildings in their own name, nor can they open their bank accounts with a formal name of their religious organization. Of course, it is possible to conduct cross-cultural missions without legal status. Many churches have already sent out many missionaries abroad and proceeded in creative ways. However, from a long-term perspective, it is necessary for Chinese churches to obtain legal status from the Chinese government in order to go abroad and to carry out cross-cultural missions along with the root of the Belt and Road Initiative.

Policy of Government

The attitude and policy of the Chinese government have had a profound effect on the MC 2030 movement. From the government's point of view, it will require the help and participation of Chinese churches in the Belt and Road Initiative. Participation of Chinese Christians in the Belt and Road policy will be a great help for the success of the national project. From this point of view, it is possible that the Chinese government will show a positive attitude toward the MC 2030 movement.

On the other hand, however, it is possible that the Chinese government will also show a negative attitude toward the MC movement. The Chinese government is concerned about the clash between Chinese Christianity and Islam. For example, recently two Chinese Christians have been martyred by Islamic terrorist attacks in Pakistan. Because of this incident, Chinese Muslims have been campaigning against the MC 2030 movement and Chinese Christian participation in the Belt and Road Initiative. The attitude of the Chinese government toward the MC 2030 movement is still reserved. Yet, I believe it is important for the Chinese government to have a positive attitude toward the MC movement.

RESPONSE

Increase of Participants

The MC 2030 movement is being recognized and spreading out positively. Participants are increasing inside of China and abroad. At the first conference in 2015, there were sixty partner churches, but it spread to 200 partners through the second and third conferences. More and more, domestic churches are agreeing to the vision of MC 2030 and attending movement conferences. It is quickly spreading abroad, and the number of participants in global mission agencies and Chinese diaspora churches is increasing.

Development of Creative Mission Models

As the MC movement moves forward, new and creative mission models are being formed and developed. At the second Jeju conference, I heard about the combined ministry of the Chinese churches and the two mission agencies. (Due to the sensitive nature of the current political climate in China I can't name these organizations here so I will refer to them as "O" and "P.") The O agency has served China for a long time and has strong connection with Chinese churches. On the contrary, the P agency, as a professional agency for the Islamic world, has a rich history and profound knowhow of Islamic ministry. These two agencies have collaborated on a combined ministry through their unique role sharing.

The O agency is finding human and material resources for mission through their network with Chinese churches. The O agency trains them with basic training and transfers them to the P agency for the next step. The P agency will train volunteers with its profound and professional course for Islamic ministry and dispatch them to appropriate ministries. This is a positive model that fills each organization's deficiencies through a creative alliance between Chinese churches and two mission organizations. There is room for newer, creative mission models to be developed in the future too.

Need for a Church-Planting Movement

The most basic part that should not be overlooked in the MC 2030 movement is a church-planting ministry. China's evangelization rate is only about 6-7 percent. This limited Christian population is also concentrated in rural areas. Due to the rapid urbanization of Chinese society, the rural population is decreasing and the urban population is rapidly increasing. An urban church-planting program is urgently needed in China. In addition, when Chinese Christians move to the Eurasian Continent with the Belt and Road Initiative, they are in huge need of church-planting churches for Chinese and local people. For the success of the MC 2030 movement, cross-cultural church planting is inevitable. The MC 2030 movement has to prepare strategies for cross-cultural church planting. It is necessary to cultivate church-planting experts for domestic urban cities and the cross-cultural world.

Need to Cooperate in the Field

When Chinese Christians go to mission fields on the Eurasian continent, they will need an attitude of coalition with others. There will already be mission agencies in mission fields before Chinese missionaries arrive there. For example, in Uzbekistan, they will meet Western or Korean mission organizations already working there. Existing organizations will already understand local cultures and their ministry will already be going on. If Chinese Christians humbly learn from their experience as latecomers, they can reduce mistakes and errors through the experience of the senior leader. Chinese missionaries of the MC 2030 movement should not be isolated, and there should be exchanges and cooperation among existing teams in an open manner. So they need to be trained in communication, language, and culture. Cooperation and coalition activities between the Chinese and others will help them adapt to local culture quickly and improve their ministry efficiency.

REFLECTION

I finish this case study by introducing a question and answer from the advisory meeting of the MC 2030 in February 2017, because I believe that this dialogue shows the meaning of the movement very well. Yu, who was the representative of WEC Korea, asked this question to professor Fang, who is a prominent leader in the Chinese Church and was the chairman of the third conference:

"Currently, global mission agencies have difficulties in recruiting missionaries in the Western region. During the last ten to twenty years, vacancies of Western missionaries have been filled with the missionaries of the Korean church. However, the passion of the Korean church for the mission is cooling down. In this situation, is the Chinese Church ready to participate in global mission? Are Chinese Christians ready to take on the role of finding and providing human and material resources for global mission?"

Professor Fang replied humbly and shortly: "We are not ready to join global mission. We, the Chinese Church, are willing to learn and follow God's guidance to join God's mission, but we have a long way to go. Please pray for us and help us."

This dialogue shows the current situation, crisis, and opportunity of the global mission.

The Lord calls and uses different nations and people for his mission and ministry in different ages. God is calling Chinese Christians to God's mission through the MC 2030 movement. The MC 2030 is a marvelous and bold movement raised by God. The Chinese church has brought its strong mission vision of BTJ since the early 20th century. The Belt and

Road Initiative, which is being widely promoted by the Chinese government, is now opening wide its doors for the Mission China 2030. I believe MC 2030 will become a major mission movement of the 21st century.

This movement will be a representative movement of the non-Western world in the Global South Era. God is doing amazing things on the continent of Eurasia through China. I hope you keep an eye on this extraordinary movement and join the movement for his kingdom.

CONCLUSION

GLOBAL CHURCH PLANTING

By Gregg A. Okesson

How does one wrap one's head around something as diverse, complex, and incredibly dynamic as global church planting? Not by establishing fixed models or by lifting up selected exemplars for everyone else to follow. Global church planting is appreciated less by reductionism and more by description. Hence, we gain insights into the *missio Dei* by listening to stories told by church planters all around the world. And that is precisely what *Global Voices* seeks to accomplish.

The chapters in this book have described fascinating case studies in Israel, Kenya, New Zealand, England, Montreal, Northern India, and China. The diversity of contexts unsettles any attempt to fix certain models or strategies that transcend cultural boundaries. However, rather than suggesting that every church planter is free to do as they please, these eight stories reveal similarities in the face of the tremendous differences. The chapters in this book are thus like little mosaic pieces that have integrity in their own selves, but when combined with other pieces produce a masterpiece inspiring wonder. In this conclusion, I want to reflect back upon the diverse contexts and weave together some of the common themes we've learned about global church planting. We will look at the discrete pieces, while also looking at how they contribute together to form a masterpiece.

Initially, all eight stories begin with their context. The contexts of the churches are as diverse as the church plants themselves. Each of the stories arises like a fresh, green sapling out of the rocky soil in which they were planted. We hear of urbanization in Kenya and China; tragedy (such as with the earthquakes in New Zealand); different forms of secularization (England and Montreal); socio-religious conflict arising from places such as Israel, Northern India, and China; the travails of youth (such as gangs in Columbia and suicide in New Zealand); religious forms of syncretism; colonialism and reactions against colonialism (like with the Quiet Revolution in Quebec); Hindu nationalism and the caste system; government opposition to Christianity (in Northern India and in China); and ubiquitous poverty. The different chapters read like complex interconnected puzzles, offering a dizzying array of difficulties with no identifiable way out.

But then a crack appears, and a brilliant shard of light pierces the darkness. In most of the stories, this occurs after prayer or years of waiting upon the Holy Spirit or both. It happens in different ways for each church plant: sometimes after a spiritual retreat, while in other instances through the initiation of a friend or co-worker. The early beginnings of the church plant arise in unexpected ways. But it's clear the Spirit of God is behind the work.

Another similarity found in each of the stories is the involvement of the community in the planting process. We don't hear of heroic individual leaders working alone. In some cases, a singular catalyst contributes a leading role in the early beginnings of the church plant. But each of the stories describes with great pains the collaborative work of a diverse community, such as what occurred in New Zealand and North India. The "house church" movement in China offers the best example, and should demand more attention given to community-based church planting as we analyze what the Spirit of God is doing around the world. In the West, we've often focused upon a singular "planter" (from our cultural value of individualism), but each of the stories compels us to look at how communities plant churches around the world.

Another commonality is that most of the churches highlighted in this book plant other churches (such as in Israel, Kenya, North India, and China). Hence, we're given the privilege of analyzing up close the DNA of churches that reproduce themselves. It's clear that each of the congregations begins with a broader vision than planting just one church. While the different authors don't talk extensively about the *missio Dei* as it relates to their church-planting efforts, it's clear the community of authors represented in this book sees itself within that larger theological mission of what God is accomplishing in the world. For future case study work, more analysis needs to be given to *how* and *why* churches plant other churches, and especially those crossing cultural boundaries. In a couple of the chapters, we're exposed to cross-cultural church planting (like with Israel and North India), and we need more examples of what this looks like, and how global churches are planting so effectively. Personally, I would like to see a subsequent collection of case studies in cross-cultural church planting around the world that offers these addendums to what we find here.

Each of these churches likewise influences their community. They don't just exist for "saving souls" but they also witness to larger social constructs around the church, such as ethnicity or the needs of people "at risk" (such as suicide and foster care in New Zealand, or gangs in Colombia). The fact that many of the chapters write openly about poverty, religious conflict, ethnicity, and the social needs of people living in the region (or some combination of these) illustrates that their congregations are well-positioned—both theologically and sociologically—to face these larger realities. More attention needs to be given to *how* churches witness to the public realm. In the West, we often paint maps of the cosmos through Enlightenment binaries of "private/public," "sacred/secular." However, different chapters in this book illustrate that the global church moves fluidly between these binaries; or as Harri Englund says of African Christianity, "Ideas expressed in, and actions taken within, apparently different domains and institutions feed into each other, and what belongs to the public sphere or the private spheres is to be investigated and not assumed."[1] Hence, greater attention needs to be given to how global churches move fluidly between what happens inside the congregation with how they relate to public realities outside the church.

Finally, let me offer a few observations about what the authors include (or don't include) in their narratives. I find it interesting that some of the case studies begin with a carefully detailed financial strategy (such as Israel, Kenya, and Montreal), while others make no mention of finances (China and North India). Some of this could be due to the person narrating the case study (and what is important to him or her). Alternatively, the inclusion (or omission) of finances might be due to the kinds of churches being planted, where "house churches" require fewer financial resources, let's say, than "remissioning" traditional cathedrals in Montreal. The absence of finances in some of the case studies shouldn't suggest that they don't need resources, just that they have chosen to place their emphasis on different aspects. I also found it interesting that a few of the chapters (such as Case Study 4 in North of England) discuss at length church planting in other locations outside a traditional building, while for others this didn't seem to be a critical part of their church-planting strategy. We need to interrogate whether this was due to a Western reaction against the privatization of Christianity, or as with the examples in India and China, if it is naturally understood that churches in these countries could not meet in any recognized building (and thus was never mentioned).

Most of the churches likewise operate out of an established denominational structure. But a few of them show creativity in adapting the structure to a new vision of church planting. We see this especially in Montreal and North of England and how each of these congregations reflects renewal movements taking place within the Church of England in relation to church planting. They are constantly rethinking their structures. Meanwhile the case study in Northern India reveals a new denomination coming into being. It's become fashionable in missional circles to criticize denominations and structures for how they impede church planting, but the chapters in this book offer interesting examples of how the global church is using, adapting, and even creating new ecclesiastical structures in the process of robust forms of church planting.

The eight chapters in this book are incredibly diverse. We can't reduce them to a couple models, or wrap our heads around them as if "to figure them out." This is the noted advantage of using a case-study approach for studying global church planting. Our intention in this book is less prescriptive and more descriptive. However, by describing first, we can then tease out some of the broader lessons learned by studying global church planting for how it might benefit others all around the world. We hope this book is a gift to others who share a common desire to see church planting continue to bear fruit in diverse cultural contexts.

I hope you've enjoyed this rare opportunity of walking onto the scene of eight church plants from around the world, learning from their successes and failures. As World Christianity continues to blossom, we need more books such as this one which take the reader by the hand into the incredible diversity and beauty of global church planting. At the conclusion of this book, it's easy to marvel at God's mission in the world and how he's accomplishing it through the planting of congregations as witnesses to the activity of the Father, Son, and Holy Spirit.

ENDNOTES

Introduction

1. See Phillip Jenkins, *The Next Christendom: The Coming of Global Christianity* (New York: Oxford University Press, 2011). A helpful short introduction to the rise of global Christianity is Lamin Sanneh, *Whose Religion is Christianity? The Gospel Beyond the West* (Grand Rapids, MI: Wm. B. Eerdmans Publishing, 2003).
2. For a quick overview of global Christianity see the "Status of Global Christianity, 2017, in the Context of 1900-2050" from the Center for the Study of Global Christianity at Gordon-Conwell Theological Seminary, http://www.gordonconwell.edu/ockenga/research/documents/StatusofGlobalChristianity2017.pdf.
3. http://www.pewforum.org/2011/12/19/global-christianity-exec/. Generally speaking, the Global North includes the United States, Canada, Europe, as well as Australia and New Zealand. The Global South is made up of Africa, Latin America, and Asia, including the Middle East.
4. See Timothy Tennent, *Invitation to World Missions: A Trinitarian Missiology for the Twenty-first Century* (Grand Rapids, MI: Kregel, 2010), 31.
5. Ibid, 37.
6. Martin Robinson, *Planting Mission-Shaped Churches Today* (Oxford, UK: Monarch Books, 2006), 144.
7. John Stott, *Christian Mission in the Modern World* (Downers Grove, IL: InterVarsity, 1975).

Case Study 1

1. The Alpha Course is a program for Christ seekers created by the HTB Church in London, England, to address specific issues related to the Christian faith. It is now used around the world.

2. *Basuco* is an inexpensive cocaine paste which uses the dust scraped from the clay bricks as a base to be smoked in cigar form with either tobacco or marijuana.

3. *The Story* is a chronological organization of the Bible divided into 31 chapters. The *Camino de Vida* church used it as a part of their discipleship programing in 2015 and 2016 (Grand Rapids, MI: Zondervan, 2010).

4. Seventy-five percent of Colombia's population is urban. (Atlantic Council) Medellín has a population of 3.5 million people.

5. Carolina Moreno, "Medellín, Colombia Named 'Innovative City of The Year' in *WSJ* and Citi Global Competition," *The Huffington Post*, March 2, 2013, https://www.huffpost.com/entry/medellin-named-innovative-city-of-the-year_n_2794425, accessed April 27, 2017.

6. Jeremy McDermott, "20 Years After Pablo: The Evolution of Colombia's Drug Trade," InSight Crime | Organized Crime In The Americas, December 3, 2013, http://www.insightcrime.org/news-analysis/20-years-after-pablo-the-evolution-of-colombias-drug-trade, accessed May 16, 2017.

7. According to a Pew Research Study, 79 percent of the Colombian population professes to be Catholic and a growing 13 percent are Protestant, a large portion of which are Pentecostal. The study also shows Protestants are about twice as likely to practice their faith as are Catholics. See Benjamin Wormald, "Religion in Latin America," Pew Research Center's Religion & Public Life Project (November 12, 2014), accessed April 27, 2017, http://www.pewforum.org/2014/11/13/religion-in-lat- in-america/.

8. Syncretism is the combination of two different religious practices— in this case Christianity and folk-religion. The problem is that it unites them without a critical examination that would result in contextualization.

9. Split-level Christianity arises when the Christian faith is relegated to a narrow portion of people's lives.

10. In the early 1960s, some Latin American theologians saw the need for a theological response to widespread conditions of poverty and injustice. Their concerns took a relatively consistent theological

shape, which made a strong impact on the Roman Catholic Church at the Second General Conference of the Latin American Episcopate (CELAM), held in Medellín, Colombia, in 1968. At that conference, the current historical situation in Latin America was recognized as one of oppression, poverty, and liberation. The church was called to denounce the oppression and side with the forces struggling for liberation, Daniel G. Reid, R. D. Linder, B.L. Shelley, H.S. Stout, Dictionary of Christianity in America (Downers Grove, IL: Intervarsity Press, 1990). In 1972, a religious movement began, especially among Roman Catholic clergy in Latin America, that combines political philosophy usually of a Marxist orientation with a theology of salvation as liberation from injustice, Merriam-Webster, I. Merriam-Webster's Collegiate Dictionary, 11th ed. (Springfield, MA: Merriam-Webster, Inc., 2003). See also Phillip Berryman, Liberation Theology (Oak Park, Ill.: Meyer Stone Books, 1987), 22-24, and Stephen B. Bevans and Roger P. Schroeder, Constants in Context: A Theology of Mission for Today (Maryknoll, NY: Orbis Books, 2004), 312.

11. The Colombian Constitution of 1991 guaranteed freedom of religion and removed the Catholic Church as the official religion of Colombia. See "República de Colombia Republic of Colombia Constitución de 1991 con reformas hasta 2005 Political Constitution of 1991 through 2005 reforms," Colombia: Constitución de 1991, con Reformas hasta 2005, accessed May 5, 2017, http://pdba.georgetown.edu/Constitutions/Co- lombia/col91. html#mozTocId49987.

12. This can be attributed to the American missionary movement that greatly influenced Latin America. Early nineteenth-century revivals awakened the missionary movements that gave birth to the first evangelical churches in Latin America. The initial belief was that the missionary's role was to proclaim the gospel and social transformation would take place automatically when individuals were converted. Over time, theological liberalism and secularism in the United States influenced the evangelical movement in such a way that spiritual transformation was separated from social transformation. The two main emphases of the church were to

win "souls" and plant churches. Attempts to address social issues were viewed as contrary to a very personalized gospel. In fact, social concern was equated with liberal thinking. Over time, dispensational teaching supported this dichotomy between the spiritual and the social. The Scofield Bible, which proliferated throughout the continent, was a primary carrier of that teaching. José Míguez Bonino, in his book *Faces of Latin American Protestantism* of 1995, discusses this more thoroughly.

13. The prosperity gospel is a movement that arose within charismatic evangelical churches during the early 1970s, stressing the power of faith in obtaining the divine blessings of physical health and financial prosperity.

14. In August 2016, Catholic and Protestants alike organized marches and sit-ins in over twenty Colombian cities in support of traditional family values as a response to the Department of Education's new sex-education curriculum, which included topics such as alternative lifestyles, gender neutrality, and other controversial topics that contradict biblical teaching. They also came together on both sides of the vote to ratify the government's peace treaty with the Revolutionary Armed Forces of Colombia (known by the Spanish acronym FARC), the primary guerrilla group and opponent to the government in the country's civil war that began in 1964.

15. Nominalism is the view that neither universals nor essences are real. That is, they have no extra-mental existence. Everything is particular.

16. Nüesch-Olver, Delia, "Home." Home - Latin America Area - Free Methodist World Missions in Latin America, https://latinamericaarea.com/, accessed April 27, 2017.

17. Dr. Gómez currently serves as a part-time professor at the Fundación Seminario Bíblico de Colombia. He supports the denomination through pastoral education and church planting with the other part of his time.

18. Leal, John Jairo. Interview by Beth Gómez. Personal Conversations. Medellín, April 26, April 28 and May 6, 2017. Unless otherwise indicated, the majority of information about

Camino de Vida church and its corresponding groups, or comments attributed to Leal were obtained during these interviews.

19. Both Leal and Castro have degrees in theology from the Fundación Universitaria Seminario Bíblico de Colombia (FUSBC, 2007, 2008).

20. The city of Medellín is divided into sixteen *comunas* for local management.

21. Patiño, Rossemberg. Interview by Beth Gómez. Personal Conversations. Medellín, May 9, 11, and 12, 2017. Unless otherwise indicated, the information about the *Robledo Pelicanos* group in this case study was obtained from these conversations.

22. Perez, Luis Fernando. Interview by Beth Gómez. Personal Conversations. Medellín, May 5, 12, and 13, 2017. All of the information from Perez throughout this document was obtained during these interviews.

23. Castrillon, Juan Ricardo. Interview by Beth Gómez. Personal Conversations. Medellín, May 7 and 8, 2017. All of the information about *Movimiento Renovación* or from Castrillon throughout this document was obtained during these interviews.

24. Bennett, Bruce, "Methodology." Community Church Planting. https://www.ccp.international/, accessed May 3, 2017.

25. In May 2016, the school where the church met asked it to move to another location. *Camino de Vida* moved to a more central location and now meets in a movie theater on Sunday mornings.

26. According to The Consultancy for Human Rights and Displacement (CODHES), forced displacement implies the loss of lands, belongings, families, friends, social, economic, and family networks, and undermines cultural roots and personal projects (CODHES, 2004, El Desplazamiento en Cifras, www.codhes.org.co/cifras.php). CODHES points out that 97.6 percent of the households registered in the United Register of Displaced Population (RUPD) are below the poverty line, and 96 percent are non-registered persons. In addition, 78.8 percent of the households enrolled in the RUPD live below the indigence line.

27. The church-planting budget comes from the Colombia Country Share account that is divided to support the ministry of the Free

Methodist Church throughout the country. Funds for this account are donations received from the US. While there is an annual goal for this budget, the Colombian Board of Administration acts on faith when allocating the funds.

Case Study 2

1. According to the UN, 55 percent of the world's population lives in urban areas, a proportion that is expected to increase to 68 percent by 2050. The *2018 Revision of World Urbanization Prospects* produced by the Population Division of the UN Department of Economic and Social Affairs (UN DESA) notes that future increases in the size of the world's urban population are expected to be highly concentrated in just a few countries. Together, India, China and Nigeria will account for 35 percent of the projected growth of the world's urban population between 2018 and 2050. By 2050, it is projected that India will have added 416 million urban dwellers, China 255 million and Nigeria 189 million. See the UN Report, https://www.un.org/development/desa/en/news/population/2018-revision-of-world-urbanization-prospects.html.

2. Aylward Shorter, and Edwin Onyancha, *Secularism in Africa* (Nairobi: Paulines Publications Africa, 1997), 32.

3. Niemeyer, Larry, *Summary of the Nairobi Church Survey* (Nairobi: Daystar University College, 1989), 11.

4. Ibid, 20.

5. Grigg, Viv, *Cry of the Urban Poor* (Monrovia CA: MARC, 1992), 275.

6. Burnette C. Fish and Gerald W. Fish, *The Place of Songs: A History of the World Gospel Mission and the Africa Gospel Church in Kenya* (Nairobi: General Printers Ltd., 1989), 376.

7. Niemeyer, Larry, *Summary of the Nairobi Church Survey* (Nairobi: Daystar University College, 1989), 17-18.

8. After much prayer and consultation, the following were selected to form the first church-planting team of the church: Gideon Kiongo (acting chairman), Esther Njenga (acting secretary), Patrick

Murunga, Beatrice Murunga, Lee Weiss, Sandy Weiss, and Nahum Mensah Jr.

9. Weiss, Sarah, *Minutes of the Church Planting Team* (Nairobi: Good Shepherd Africa Gospel Church, 1990).

10. Those who were recruited in this phase included Caleb and Fresky Kiplagat, Wayne and Sally Dye, Samuel Odote, Mwangati Mwendabose, Edwin Kirui, Esther, Ngina, Zipporah Itotia, Gladys Itotia, Nancy Musonik, Agnes Musonik, and Stephen Amadalo.

Case Study 3

1. In 2005, the World Christian Database (WCD) ranked New Zealand fourteenth in the "Most Non-Religious Nations" category at 20.3 percent. All other countries ranked before fourteen were non-English speaking and mostly former communist countries. In comparison, Australia was ranked twenty (15.2 percent), United Kingdom twenty-seven (12.3 percent), Canada twenty-nine (12.2 percent), United States thirty-seven (9.3 percent), and South Africa sixty-seven (3.1 percent).

2. For more information about Skylight and/or the WAVES program, see: http://skylight.org.nz/Waves.

3. See Mike Breen and 3DM missional discipleship movement: https://3dmovements.com/.

Case Study 4

1. The draft name for this church plant was "Next Generation Church;" this was later changed to "G2."

2. For an up-to-date overview of the Fresh Expression of Church movement see *Encountering the Day of Small Things* by George Lings.

3. The Cathedral and Metropolitan Church of Saint Peter in York, commonly known as "York Minster."

4. A passage in the life of St. John of Beverley (who was a bishop from 705–718) written by Folcard, a Flemish monk at Thorney Abbey, and dedicated to Archbishop Ealdred, refers to the saint using the church.

5. Wimber was the founding leader of the Vineyard Church movement.

6. alt:worship is a term first used in the 1990s and refers to experimental forms of congregational worship inspired by the culture of UK night-clubs.

7. See "From the Margins to the Mainstream: New Churches in York" in *Church Growth in Britain* by David Goodhew for a more detailed description.

8. MinDiv, the national body of the Church of England that oversees ordained vocations, estimates that G2 has produced ordinands at more than ten times the national parish average by congregation size.

9. For example, G2 has been featured in five books and three Ph.D. dissertations.

10. See https://www.churchofengland.org/sites/default/files/2017-11/everyonecounts_keyfindings.pdf, accessed April 28, 2017.

11. For example, the term "Missing Generation" was used in an Evangelical Alliance Council meeting in September 2009.

12. It is estimated that less than ten people in the last thirteen years have moved from another local church to join G2.

13. Authors William Strauss and Neil Howe are widely credited with naming the "millennials," a term they coined in 1987, identifying the prospective link to the new millennium of the high school graduating class of 2000. See *Millennials Rising: The Next Great Generation.*

14. "Older" here refers to people over thirty-five years of age.

15. Some suggest there are two missional modes of church: "you come to us" or "we go to you." For example, see Pete Ward in *Youthwork and the Mission of God: Frameworks for Relational Outreach.* The attractional model is an example of "you come to us" evangelism.

16. For one definition of "attractional church" see *Shaping of Things to Come, The: Innovation and Mission for the 21st-Century Church* by Alan Hirsch.

17. This was illustrated by asking clergy at a deanery chapter meeting. Of twenty-two clergy, only two had received personal mentoring before entering theological college.
18. For example, this was observed by one G2 ordinand who on attending a preaching class at theological college was surprised to find that he had preached more than twenty sermons, but most of his fellow students had preached one or none.
19. For more on the decline in biblical literacy amongst millennials see *The Bible Reading of Young Evangelicals: An Exploration of the Ordinary Hermeneutics and Faith of Generation Y* by Ruth Perrin (Pickwick Publications, 2016).
20. This young leader is now a highly valued speaker who speaks regularly at national events and is being trained for ordained ministry in the Church of England as a prospective church planter.
21. It seems that "leading from the middle" is a phrase recently used in teaching and education, though it is used distinctively here.
22. This "two-hand" illustration is attributed to the controversial preacher Mark Driscoll.
23. For example, see "The Declaration of Assent" which is made by deacons, priests, and bishops of the Church of England when they are ordained and, on each occasion, when they take up a new appointment (Canon C 15): "The Church of England is part of the One, Holy, Catholic and Apostolic Church, worshipping the one true God, Father, Son and Holy Spirit. It professes the faith uniquely revealed in the Holy Scriptures and set forth in the catholic creeds [closed hand], which faith the Church is called upon to proclaim afresh in each generation [open hand]."
24. Some churches have taken to calling the child-to-late-20s age range "younger years" in order to give a positive label to an older threshold of spiritual adulthood.
25. A multi-site church is one church that meets at multiple locations.

Case Study 6

1. Tim Daykin, "Closed church buildings re-open with new purposes." *BBC News*, 25 May 2010, http://news.bbc.co.uk/local/hampshire/hi/people_and_places/religion_and_ethics/newsid_8700000/8700180.stm.
2. See Behiels, Michael D., *Prelude to Quebec's Quiet Revolution: Liberalism vs Neo-Nationalism, 1945–60* (1985).
3. See the Holy Trinity Brompton Story at https://www.htb.org/our-story.

Case Study 7

1. Paul Harris, *International to Global Justice (Edinburgh Studies in World Ethics)* (Edinburgh: Edinburgh University Press, 2010), 124.

Case Study 8

1. For more information see https://backtojerusalem.com.
2. Please see https://www.worldbank.org/en/country/china/overview.
3. For a more in depth discussion on the Belt Road and its implications for evangelism in China see the following article https://thediplomat.com/2018/07/chinas-belt-and-road-exporting-evangelism/. See also https://www.chinasource.org/resource-library/articles/back-to-jerusalem-a-moving-history.
4. The use of the word "Club" is code for church/house fellowship.
5. Use https://www.christianitytoday.com/edstetzer/2016/october/diaspora-missions-diaspora-churches-as-equal-partners-in-mi.html.

Conclusion

1. Harri Englund, "Introduction," In Englund (ed.) *Christianity and Public Culture in Africa* (Athens, OH: Ohio University Press, 2011), 1-24: 2.

IN THEIR OWN WORDS:

Struggles and Lessons from Global Church Planters

While the case studies above come from only eight writers, we interviewed more than sixty of the church-planting leaders who attended the Global Summit from the countries of Nepal, India, Kenya, Nigeria, Israel, Singapore/Indonesia, Philippines, Columbia, Brazil, Costa Rica, England, Ireland, New Zealand, United States, Canada, and South Korea, asking them the following two questions:

1. What are the top three to five unique and personal struggles that church planters face in your context and country of origin?
2. What lessons and principles have you learned that promote church planter health and spiritual vitality?

Find below their answers, which offer profound insight into both the struggles that church planters face and the lessons that they have learned, which promote health and spiritual vitality.

I. STRUGGLES CHURCH PLANTERS FACE

Israel

- Opposition: A planter has to deal with 1700 years of antipathy between the Jewish people and the church.
- Rejection: Judaism, Islam, and traditional Christianity are generally suspicious of or threatened by evangelicals in Israel (or they feel

both). Additionally, Jewish followers of Jesus are generally regarded as traitors to Judaism and the Jewish race.

- Insecurity: For example, landlords do their best to avoid renting their properties to evangelicals, and especially Jewish followers of Jesus.
- Financial stress: Israel is one of the most expensive countries in the world.
- A competitive spirit: Other pastors can regard a new plant as competition and an impediment to their success.

Brazil

- Lack of specific church-planting training.
- Not enough financial support from the established local churches.
- Loneliness, especially in the first years on the field; other pastors have the church members and fellow pastors nearby.

New Zealand

- Secular context influences plant team phase—quantity and quality is affected with the result that planters start with less personnel resource around them and greater personal load than is desirable.
- Financial resources are limited, often requiring bi-vocational church planters to plant a) alone and without staff support and b) part time
- Geographical isolation can lead to personal isolation.
- Personal emotional resilience is significantly tested in plant situations and is exacerbated by the above factors.

Singapore/Indonesia

- Education for children to fulfill government requirements (Singapore).
- Indigenous leadership transition (Indonesia and Singapore).

- Rise of radicalization and extremism of religion especially Islam (Indonesia and Singapore).
- Legal place of worship—government policies prohibiting gathering of Christians (Indonesia and Singapore).

India

- Opposition and persecution.
- Poverty and financial struggles.
- Educating their children.
- Covering distant villages by walking or cycling, especially in hilly areas.
- Lack of medical facilities nearby.

Canada

- The median age of church members is in the 70s.
- Churches are not working from an established set of practices that highlight effectives steps toward renewal.
- Many Christians seem to have lost the ability to relearn how to inhabit a new missional landscape that lives at the edge rather than at the center of society. Thus, our church planters experience being pulled into an extended period of grief and bewilderment as the church responds to its own losses of privilege, resources, and status.
- Outdated industrial employment systems of leadership formation lead to lack of creativity and entrepreneurship. Our church leaders have been initially trained in the skills of managing the internal life of a church/organization. Missional leadership implies leading the church in external mission activity beyond the church walls. We need a pathway that seeks to equip a new type of Christian leader who can pursue these challenges for mission, preferably within the context of Church planting, Fresh Expressions, etc.

England

- Lack of support and understanding of church planting by senior people, such as Bishops and Diocesan staff.
- Not much money available to help start new churches (except for some limited models).
- Few or no support systems for pioneers.
- Low appetite for risk in the national church and among bishops.

Nepal

- Discipleship: Providing discipleship is a big personal struggle for the church planter, especially in rural settings.
- Insecurity: Due to freshly-banned religious conversion after 2015, there are high feelings of fear of persecution, especially in leadership circles.
- Due to limited resources, multiplication has been negatively affected.
- Infrastructure development: Holding church in Nepal is still in an illegal status. So attaining government property is a big challenge for developing infrastructure. This situation has made church vulnerable with low social esteem.
- Finances: As Church members come from a moderate family background, they are not mature enough to provide support even to their pastors, so pastors are usually bi-vocational.

Ireland

- Resilience: Church planting in Europe/Ireland is hard work.
- Resources: People, finance, and accommodation.
- Leadership: Lack of trained mature Christians to lead the work.
- Secularism/Materialism/Post-Modernism.
- Scandals in the established Roman Catholic Church.
- Young people/millennials have turned away from church.

Kenya

- Senior leaders without an understanding that obedience to the Great Commission unleashes Holy Spirit power, which is the energy source for the operation of the Body of Christ.
- Lack of mentors skilled in empowering disciple makers to be followers of Jesus.
- Inadequate training for building a team who can start, operate, and maintain a movement.
- Insufficient training and authority to recruit and engage the resources needed to start, operate, and maintain a movement or project.
- Tribalism and cultural isolation (of all ethnicities and classes) preventing cross-cultural and cross-class evangelism (i.e., failure to imitate John 1:14).
- Tradition, which discourages new approaches and new leadership people, styles, and systems.

England

- The deeply secularized and anti-Christian posture of a post-Christendom culture, and the deeply secularized life of most mainline liberal denominations who act as a counter-witness to planting radical Christian community.
- The general lack of spiritual zeal among Christians, even those who think of themselves as pioneers who may see what is needed but lack willingness to count the cost of discipleship necessary to follow through.
- The temptation to substitute authentic disciple-making community with programmatic approaches to church planting.
- The lack of depth in personal spirituality among church leaders, and widespread ignorance about how to practice the presence of God and respond to his movements in the world.
- The general lack of teaching on the person and work of the Spirit, including discernment about the role of both fruit and gifts of the Spirit in equipping us for participation in the mission of God.

Colombia

- Economic resources: Most people live on minimal wages, trying to put food on the table and be faithful to God's call.
- Lack of trust: Small circles of evangelicals have damaged the reputation of the church—some using the prosperity gospel to enrich themselves, others aligning with political agendas, and still others engaging in inappropriate or illegal sexual behaviors. The news reports these, and people are slow to trust evangelical Christians.
- Changing paradigms: Buildings provide identity and a meeting place, but the new model we are using is based on the community of believers rather than places. This creates tension as we retrain our thinking.

United States

- The greatest challenge is identifying and equipping young spiritual entrepreneurs. We are challenged to equip them in a way that doesn't burden them with debt but provides foundational theological training and quickly releases them to engage.
- Another challenge is encouraging new expressions that are different than traditional church. Creative, innovative faith communities are especially appealing to ethnic minorities and young people.
- A shift in attitude with our established healthy congregations. This church-planting movement requires healthy churches to adopt a mentality of multiplication, seeding new churches and releasing laity to start new ministries.

Costa Rica

- Tradition over Scripture: Since our area is considered to be a Catholic region, there is already some idea of what a church is supposed to "look like." This creates some skepticism when you are doing church in a "different way."

- A huge challenge is to avoid the temptation of "leaders" from other churches coming over to push their agendas onto the new church plant. Sometimes this may be done by confusing new believers with non-biblical theology.
- Another personal challenge is feeling that you are the only one doing what you are doing at times. When you are doing something to reach the people that have not been reached before, you have to be creative about what puts you in a "different" category from other religious leaders.

Nigeria

- Church planters face the menace of insurgency, especially the dreaded Boko Haram and the Fulani Herdsmen (otherwise known as "gunmen"). This makes the environment of church planting extremely difficult.
- To worsen the situation, some of the believers are going back to syncretism in order to deal with the situation.
- Economic hardship is another difficulty church planters go through.
- This affects the education of a church planter's children.
- Yet another issue is doing a paradigm shift in church planting, such as underground church planting. Most church denominations are not conversant with such a paradigm shift. Still another issue is that of developing viable church-planting teams.

2. LESSONS LEARNED THAT PROMOTE HEALTH AND VITALITY

Kenya

- Assemble a team of Holy Spirit-anointed leaders who share the same vision for people in the same ethnicity, circumstance, or geography.
- Facilitate like-minded leaders to agree on a statement of vision, which describes the future outcomes or circumstances that will happen if they accomplish what God is calling them to do.

- Facilitate like-minded leaders to agree on a statement of mission (purpose) of what they will do to accomplish the statement of vision.
- Agree on goals by which the achievement of the statement of mission can be measured.
- Establish a prayer wall around the goals so that the attacks of the Enemy (which will come) don't defeat the health of the movement.
- Enlist partners who are willing to invest their time, talents, and treasures in the achievement of the statement of vision.

United States

Church planters struggle with personal spiritual vitality unless they have established a plan for personal devotion, ongoing spiritual formation, and renewal. Much of our equipping focuses on planting skills but neglects assisting planters to establish a system of personal devotions—which includes journaling and a dedicated accountability partner. These spiritual practices must be mobile for church planters. Planned facilitated and non-facilitated spiritual retreats have proven to support church planters. If this is not addressed as a daily rhythm early in the equipping process, it is difficult to establish.

Costa Rica

- A healthy growth balance between "head, heart, and hands," meaning taking time to grow and learn not just by the experience on the field but also by reading and studying.
- If you can't live it, don't preach it! Most people in our area have heard the message of the gospel, so now, they want to see it.
- Taking time to rest in God! Being on the field, there is always "something to do." Keeping in mind that we are not about speed in ministry but about looking for fruit that lasts.

Philippines

- First of all, they must understand the principle of self-care where they learn to look to God, first and foremost, for their needs.

- Being sent by their home church, along with the pastoral care that comes with it, is critical.
- Also, as far as training, we learned that it is best to just give them enough to get them through the first two years, and then provide ongoing training afterwards—instead of cramming everything before they leave.

India

- Holding frequent fellowship meetings.
- Conducting regular seminars on relevant biblical topics and renewing strategies on church planting and church growth.
- Holding monthly get together meetings of field level pastors and church planters for fellowship, prayers, and evaluation of the work.
- Conducting annual pastors conferences.
- Equipping them to equip others in the churches.

Columbia

- We are implementing Wesley's model of "bands," where we are providing discipleship/accountability/vision sharing/prayer, emotional, spiritual support. We meet every week for 1.5 hours to open our hearts, share our minds, pray for each other, and encourage one another in addition to casting vision and giving reports of what is happening.
- Ensuring that leaders are healthy in three areas: "Heart" (correct rhythms in life with work and rest, they are physically, relationally, emotionally, and spiritually healthy), "head" (they have a solid biblical and Wesleyan foundation), and "hands" (their ministry is fruitful... they really minister to people, they evangelize, and they are practical and not only theoretical). They must mobilize those under their leadership to do likewise.

Brazil

- Reminding them through words and specific actions that church planting is an essential element for the promotion of God's Kingdom.
- Gathering church planters and their families together for sharing their experiences with each other.
- Continually supplying them with literature and strategic material for their work on the field.
- Continually supporting them with prayer, and letting them know we are doing so.

Nepal

- Trusting God: As a believer of the living and an invisible God, I have learned to love, listen, and trust him above all else.
- Being faithful: As a faithful steward of God, I have learned to be faithful and content with little, expecting to be worthy of a big thing.
- Personal walk with God: Worshipping God daily and witnessing for Christ in season and out of season to the people in need of the truth—this has become a lifestyle.
- Family time with God: As shepherd of the little flock of Christ, I have learned first to lead my family into God's presence on a daily basis for their perfect physical, mental, and spiritual health.
- Daily meditation: As a pioneering church planter and a shepherd for the little flock of Christ, I have developed a habit of meditating on Scripture.

Israel

- Planters should maintain personal spiritual disciplines.
- Planters should maintain a solid relationship of support and accountability from a larger congregation or church-planting network or both.

- Planters should have solid financial backing over their first three years of operation. Otherwise, there will be stress that affects not only the congregation but also the planter's marriage.
- In the case of married couples, they should both receive training and ongoing counsel, and be engaged in the work together.
- Planters should engage with and regularly participate in gatherings involving a wider network of fellow leaders in the country.
- Planters should maintain a mentoring relationship with a pastor who has a track record of success in planting.
- Planters should pursue a kingdom perspective (i.e., they are concerned about the success of their congregation as it contributes to the overall expansion and health of the body of Christ nationally).

South Korea

- Passion and relationship with God and others.
- Learn the local context and culture.
- Make plans to reach local people through evangelism and mission.
- Cooperate and network with others for the sake of the kingdom of God.

England

- Network with like-minded church planters.
- Have a coach/mentor/spiritual director.
- Take regular timeouts for refreshment and getting perspective.
- Plant with a team/an apprentice.
- Emphasize spiritual disciplines.
- A clear vision for the life of discipleship as abiding deeply in God in order to live missionally in the world and a determination to pursue it.
- A passion for and participation in Wesleyan-style fellowship bands that cultivate the art of spiritual conversation through mutual accountability and spiritual guidance.

- Belonging to a wider movement of church planters among whom vision can be honed, wisdom shared, and missionary zeal can be fanned into flame.
- Establishing good rhythms of discipleship and leadership that balance both the active and contemplative aspects of ministry, including the importance of study and space for reflection.
- Submitting to the authority of a planting team to avoid the temptation of a pioneer to work as an omni-competent lone ranger and to guard against the founder's syndrome of believing they are indispensable to the mission of God.
- Strong preparation in the local church, through ministry experience, to prepare planters.
- Finding ways to bring pioneers together for mutual benefit.
- Strong mentoring of emerging younger leaders on character issues and spiritual disciplines.
- High emphasis on team models of ministry.

Singapore/Indonesia

- Embracing suffering as part of our calling.
- Concrete plans for accountability.
- Engaging in a lifelong learning journey—not just seminary training.
- Entering into strategic partnerships to ensure longevity and sustainability of ministry.

Nigeria

- Principles of dependence upon the Lord of the harvest, who gives discernment on church-planting strategies that is relevant and appropriate.
- Church planter meditation on the Word, and prayers for spiritual vitality.

- Church planter mobilizing prayer-support partners, resource-support partners, and moral-support partners, depending on the Good Shepherd who makes the sheep to lay down in green pastures.
- In addition, church planters should develop a church-planting team.
- Finally, they need rest, exercise, good dieting, and occasional medical checkups.

Canada

- It is important to have systems in place that will allow the church planter to be fully "accountable" and "supported" by an identified authority. This will enable the church planter to plan in all areas of their life (i.e., governance, operations, prayer life, finances, and healthy relationships). The church planter will know that all the identified areas will have identifiable support to enable long-term emotional, physical, and spiritual health.
- Alternative formation practices: It is vital to "infect" the system with opportunities that help form folk's imagination. These new formation practices will draw together folks who believe we are living in the richest age of mission our church has ever seen for forming and multiplying disciples.

APPENDIX 2

STUDY GUIDE

W. Jay Moon

CASE STUDY 1: CHRISTIAN MOBILIZATION IN MEDELLÍN
Free Methodist Church Planting Movement, Colombia

1. Instead of desiring to be a solo church planter, explain how the Gomez family formed a church-planting team. What various gifts and training did the different team members add?
2. While many church plants start as small home groups, the Community Church Planting (CCP) model stresses regularly adding new small groups. How are the small group leaders trained? What expectations do churches have for these leaders?
3. Consider how people like Rodriguez (the chef by training) used his marketplace context to live out his missional calling. How can the church identify and equip people like this to be church planters in the marketplace? Consider options like bi-vocational (also called "co-vocational"), business chaplains, entrepreneurial church-planting options, etc.
4. Instead of people finding their identity through their geographical neighborhood alone, in the 21st century, people often identify with others at places of work, play, and social media. How have church planters like Perez engaged these contexts for church planting in Medellín?

5. How has the "prosperity gospel" affected church planting? How should church planters respond in a way that provides a biblical perspective on both the potential good and harm in wealth and encourages the flourishing of society? What has helped you personally to have a balanced and biblical perspective on wealth, faith, and work?

CASE STUDY 2: KENYA'S URBAN CHALLENGE
Good Shepherd Africa Gospel Church, Nairobi

1. While many statistics are cited for the tremendous growth of Christianity in Africa, what did the Good Shepherd Church find by their research about the need for church planting in Nairobi? How did this background research affect their decision to plant a church?
2. What surprise did the new church plant experience on the first day of worship at their new site? What did they learn from this?
3. Consider their various efforts at outreach and evangelism. What were the results from these efforts and what did their team learn as a result?
4. Even though the mother church stopped providing financial support after one year, the Good News Church continued to financially survive. How did they accomplish this?

CASE STUDY 3: RAISING CHURCHES FROM RUBBLE
The Well Church, New Zealand

1. The core leadership team changed drastically over time. What factors caused this change and how did the team respond?
2. Church planters in a secular society often need to overcome people's indifference to church. How did this church plant overcome "an undercurrent of skepticism and resistance" from the local people? How did the church planting team adjust their metrics accordingly?
3. How do various styles of leadership affect church-planting teams? What role does the local culture play in determining the appropriate leadership style for a particular church plant?

4. Church planting can take a toll on the planters—emotionally, physically, and spiritually. What lessons did this team learn about preparing planters and helping them navigate the difficulties of planting? What have you found (personally or by watching others) to be the most helpful advice for maintaining a flourishing lifestyle amidst struggles?

CASE STUDY 4: RECLAIMING THE MISSING GENERATION
G2, North of England

1. The Fresh Expressions movement focuses on reaching unchurched and de-churched folks through missional experiments. What experiments and innovations did G2 attempt in order to contextualize a worship experience for unchurched and de-churched folks, particularly among millennials?
2. How has the apprenticeship model created both challenges and opportunities for the development of young leaders within the church? How has this been received inside both the church and the denomination?
3. Describe what the author means by "leading from the middle" and how this relates to the leadership and training of young leaders.
4. While G2 is applauded for attracting many de-churched millennials, there is a shortage of people over fifty years of age. What challenges does this present for the church? What do you suggest they do to address this?

CASE STUDY 5: BRINGING THE GOSPEL HOME
King of King's Ministries, Israel

1. When Wayne and his young family felt called to plant a church, they were already engaged in a successful and satisfying ministry. God often asks us to step outside of our comfort zone. What steps of faith might God be calling you to take today? How might Wayne's example encourage you to do so?

2. Wayne described that many Jews considered the Christian message an existential threat and rejected it right away. How did Wayne and his church planting team overcome this strong resistance?

3. Many churches use their buildings mostly on Sundays and Wednesday nights. How has King of King's Ministries creatively utilized their church space in order to more fully utilize their facility throughout the week for kingdom purposes? How has this engagement in the marketplace affected the church? What about its effect on the community?

4. What did they learn from the mistakes they made with the various church plants and what changes did they make for future church plants?

CASE STUDY 6: A COMMUNITY-FORWARD APPROACH
St. Jax, Montreal

1. While many church planters struggle to find a church building, there are several old church buildings in risk of closure in the UK and Canada. How has Holy Trinity Brompton responded to this opportunity? What has been the result?

2. Graham describes the pain of closing a church but also recognizes the great opportunity to reopen the church with fresh vision. Why is it sometimes necessary to close the existing church so that it can be re-started?

3. What obstacles did St. Jax face and how did they overcome them?

4. How has St. Jax used her building and location to become a "thriving hub of community-based activities" as well as a church?

5. Consider the delicate dance of evangelism in the very socially liberal and secular society of Quebec. While direct evangelistic outreaches may be resisted, how has St. Jax found ways to "become good news" in order to share the Good News in Quebec? How do you suggest that St. Jax protect itself from "mission drift" so that it does not simply become like the society where she is located?

CASE STUDY 7: MINISTERING IN THE MARGINS
Christian Evangelistic Assemblies, India

1. Church planting in unreached areas can be lonely and discouraging at times. How has the Christian Evangelistic Assemblies (CEA) team approach addressed this issue? What has been the result?
2. Ralph Winter once remarked, "Anyone who can help one hundred missionaries to the field is more important than one missionary on the field." How has the formation of the New Theological College (NTC) been a strategic step toward mobilizing church planters throughout India? On the other hand, what problems can result when students stay too long in their education process without engaging in ministry?
3. While many church plants are started in homes, how has the caste system affected people's receptivity to visiting homes? What can be done to reduce this problem?
4. Based on many social, governmental, and cultural pressures, some new believers take the position of being secret believers, like Nicodemus or Naaman, for a period of time. What are the strengths and weaknesses of this position?

CASE STUDY 8: FROM THE ENDS OF THE EARTH
Mission China 2030, China

1. While the gospel initially traveled the Roman roads to reach Europe and the Silk Road to reach China, compare this to the new Belt and Road initiative led by Chinese believers: While intended for economic growth, how does the Chinese church see this as an opportunity to bring the gospel "back to Jerusalem"? What is the same and what is different from before (e.g., consider transportation methods, government policies, diasporas, globalization, business opportunities, etc.)? What historical lessons can guide forward the church of today?
2. What are the major obstacles for the Chinese church to work in unity with other global partners, such as the Lausanne movement, mission agencies, and churches?

3. When asked if the Chinese church is ready to implement the MC 2030 initiative, Professor Fang replied humbly and shortly, "We are not ready to join global mission. We, the Chinese Church, are willing to learn and follow God's guidance to join God's mission. We have a long way to go. Please pray for us and help us." What is he saying to the global church? What are appropriate ways for churches, mission agencies, training institutions, and others to respond?

4. While large in overall number, the percentage of Christians in China is relatively small. What would you say to someone who suggested that *the Chinese church has so much internal mission and church planting to take care of that they are not able to send missionaries outside of China*? What would you say to someone who posed the same question to you and your community?

Printed in Great Britain
by Amazon